THE CASE AGAINST THE
Employee Free Choice Act

THE CASE AGAINST THE
EMPLOYEE FREE CHOICE ACT

by Richard A. Epstein

HOOVER INSTITUTION PRESS
Stanford University   Stanford, California

The Hoover Institution on War, Revolution and Peace, founded at Stanford University in 1919 by Herbert Hoover, who went on to become the thirty-first president of the United States, is an interdisciplinary research center for advanced study on domestic and international affairs. The views expressed in its publications are entirely those of the authors and do not necessarily reflect the views of the staff, officers, or Board of Overseers of the Hoover Institution.

www.hoover.org

Hoover Institution Press Publication No. 573

Hoover Institution at Leland Stanford Junior University,
Stanford, California, 94305–6010

First printing 2009
16 15 14 13 12 11 10 09   9 8 7 6 5 4 3 2 1

Manufactured in the United States of America

The paper used in this publication meets the minimum Requirements of
the American National Standard for Information Sciences—Permanence
of Paper for Printed Library Materials, ANSI/NISO Z39.48–1992. ∞

Cataloging-in-Publication Data is available from Library of Congress.

ISBN 978-0-8179-4941-9 (hardcover)
ISBN 978-0-8179-4942-6 (paperback)

Contents

PREFACE

D uring the summer of 2008, I was approached by my friend, James Franczek, senior partner at the Chicago labor law firm of Franczek, Radelet & Rose, about the proposed Employee Free Choice Act. EFCA had passed the House of Representatives in 2008, only to die in the Senate after a procedural vote to consider the bill failed to garner the necessary sixty votes. Franczek, and others with whom I met that summer, expected EFCA to be reintroduced in 2009, especially if the Democratic majority increased in the Senate and (as has turned out to be the case) Barack Obama was elected president of the United States.

President Obama, an outspoken supporter of organized labor, has taken office with solid labor-backed Democratic majorities in both the House of Representatives and the Senate. As a result, the pressure has escalated on Congress to revisit EFCA, which is surely the most controversial piece of labor legislation in the last sixty years, and perhaps since the passage of the Wagner Act in 1935. The source of the controversy lies in its three major components: an increase in the penalties for unfair labor practices (ULPs) by employers during union organization campaigns; the use of a card-check system to authorize a union for a particular bargaining unit; and a system of mandatory interest arbitration which allows a panel of federal arbitrators to set the terms of a first two-year contract if an overtly truncated time line of 130 days is not met. At the option of a union, EFCA would, in effect, bypass the protections of the secret ballot by allowing a card check to certify a union. It would thereafter deny any employer or employee the option to refuse to deal on the terms demanded by a union.

Having worked, written, and taught in the area of labor law since I was a third-year student at the Yale Law School in 1968, it took me little time to realize that this proposed legislation would have the worst possible consequences for the workplace—and through it for the overall economy. The brevity of the statute conceals many serious difficulties about its integration with existing labor laws, even as it gives evidence to the massive shift of power from private ordering to state control. Although I do not regard current labor law as ideal relative to more market-oriented approaches, it has been relatively stable on matters of collective bargaining over the past sixty years, during which it has provided a framework to which both management and labor have been able to adapt.

Shortly after I spoke with Franczek, I agreed to write a detailed study of EFCA. The task, however, was too large to do by relying solely on my own resources. I have had for several years a working affiliation with LECG consulting group, and I was able to enlist the support of one of its managing directors, Anne Layne-Farrar, with whom I have worked on many occasions. She in turn recruited one of LECG's crack research analysts, Sokol Vako, to assist me both in the collection of data and in a detailed review of the manuscript at every stage. Toward the end of the process, he was assisted by two other able research analysts, Dhiren Patki and Alina Marinova.

I have also received helpful comments from many individuals with long experience in labor law. In addition to Franczek, both David Radelet and Jennifer Niemiec of Franczek, Radelet & Rose provided me with useful background information on EFCA and card-check recognition and interest arbitration under Illinois law. Philip Miscimarra, a senior fellow at the University of Pennsylvania's Wharton School and a partner at Morgan, Lewis and Bockius, provided detailed comments on an earlier draft of this paper. Additional comments have been provided by Andrew Kramer and G. Roger King of Jones Day.

I am also grateful to my longtime friend, John Raisian, the director of the Hoover Institution, for quickly arranging the publication of this volume, and to Stephen Langlois, associate director of the Hoover Institution, for speeding this volume toward publication.

Finally, I have received financial support for this work from the Alliance to Save Main Street Jobs, which is comprised of the HR Policy Association (the leader of the Alliance), the Retail Industry Leaders Association, the Real Estate Roundtable, the American Hotel and Lodging Association, the U.S. Chamber of Commerce, the International Council of Shopping Centers, and the Associated Builders and Contractors. I am grateful for their support, and for their willingness to allow me complete freedom to write the book as I chose. I know that all members of these organizations understand that the passage of EFCA is fraught with perils not only to them as employers, but to everyone in this country, be they employer or employee. The stakes on this issue are too great to remain silent. I am honored to have this opportunity to write *The Case against the Employee Free Choice Act.*

INTRODUCTION
The EFCA Initiative

Historical Background

The Employee Free Choice Act (EFCA) is the most transformative piece of labor legislation to come before Congress since the enactment of the National Labor Relations Act of 1935 (NLRA). The NLRA marked the culmination of a systematic effort of the progressive movement that dominated so much of American intellectual life during the first third of the twentieth century. Its basic purpose was to displace the earlier judge-made regime that had previously governed labor relationships. That system did not carve out any special privileges, or impose any special burdens, on labor unions and their members. Instead, it applied the same general legal principles applicable to other forms of business and economic associations organized to advance the interests of their members. The first major departure from that model in American labor law was the passage in 1914 of section 6 of the Clayton Act, which insulated labor unions from the application of all antitrust laws insofar as their members were members of organizations "instituted for purposes of mutual help."[1] In effect,

---

1. 38 Stat. 730 (1914); 15 U.S.C. § 17. The full section reads:

§ 6 Antitrust laws not applicable to labor organizations

The labor of a human being is not a commodity or article of commerce. Nothing contained in the antitrust laws shall be construed to forbid the existence and operation of labor, agricultural, or horticultural organizations, instituted for the purpose of mutual help, and not having capital stock or conduct for profit, or to forbid or restrain individual members of such organizations from lawfully carrying out the legitimate objects thereof; nor shall such organizations, or the members thereof, be held or construed to be illegal combinations or conspiracies in restraint of trade, under the antitrust laws."

1

all efforts of workers to join together in unions were exempted from the standard antitrust law that otherwise makes horizontal arrangements between individuals a per se offense under section 1 of the Sherman Act.[2] Next, in 1926, the Railway Labor Act conferred special privileges of collective bargaining on railroad workers,[3] which were later extended to airlines.[4] Seven years later, the Norris-LaGuardia Act of 1933 placed sharp limitations on the traditional ability of employers to obtain injunctions during labor disputes.[5] Shortly thereafter, Congress passed the original version of the NLRA (the Wagner Act), which was upheld against constitutional challenges in *NLRB v. Jones & Laughlin Steel Co.*[6] Subsequent changes took place within the framework of the collective bargaining regime set out under the Wagner Act. The most important one was the Taft-Hartley Act of 1947, which cut back on some of the main advantages that the Wagner Act had conferred upon unions. Its chief innovation was to make it clear that the NLRA respected employees' collective choice on unionization, but did not put its thumb on the scale in favor of unionization if the workers voted otherwise. The original language of section 7 in the 1935 Act showed a strong preference for labor organization:

§7. Employees shall have the right to self-organization, to form, join, or assist labor organizations, to bargain collectively through

---

In addition section 20 of the Clayton Act placed limitations on the ability of courts to issue injunctions against unions or their members in various labor disputes "unless necessary to prevent irreparable injury to property, or to a property right, ..." This provision was supplanted by the Norris-LaGuardia Act, infra.

2. 26 Stat. 209 (1890), as amended, 15 U.S.C. § 1. For the early judicial response, see e.g., United States v. Hutcheson, 312 U.S. 219 (1941); United States v. American Federation of Musicians, 47 F. Supp. 304 (1942); United States v. International Hod Carriers & C. L. Dist. Council, 313 U.S. 539 (1941).

3. 44 Stat. 577 (1926), as amended, 45 U.S.C. §§ 151–188.

4. 49 Stat. 1189 (1936), 45 U.S.C. § 201.

5. 47 Stat. 70 (1932), as amended, 29 U.S.C. § 101–115.

6. The NLRB was the appellant in the case because the three circuit courts which had considered the matter had all held it unconstitutional. See, NLRB v. Jones & Laughlin Steel Corp., 1301 U.S. 1 (1937); NLRB v. Fruehauf Trailer Co., 301 U.S. 49 (1937); NLRB v.

representatives of their own choosing, and to engage in other concerted activities for the purpose of collective bargaining or other mutual aid or protection.

The Taft-Hartley Act of 1947 made explicit the converse of this proposition when it added to the above provision the following clause:

> And shall also have the right to refrain from any or all of such activities except to the extent that such right may be affected by an agreement requiring membership in a labor organization as a condition of employment as authorized in section 8(a)(3).[7]

In addition, the Taft-Hartley Act created a set of unfair labor practices with respect to union conduct which parallel those for management, including important substantive limitations on secondary boycotts, which are union actions directed against firms that did business with any employer that was the target of a union organization drive. The Taft-Hartley Act gave its explicit blessing to state right-to-work laws that allowed individuals to remain outside the union and not pay dues. These changes, however, did nothing to undo the basic principle of union elections followed by good faith bargaining between the two sides once the union was selected. Finally, the Landrum-Griffin Act of 1959[8] was directed toward issues of internal union management, with an eye to the control of union corruption—a topic outside the scope of this analysis of the EFCA.

Friedman-Harry Marks Clothing Co., 301 U.S. 58 (1937); Associated Press v. NLRB, 301 U.S. 103 (1937), and Washington, Virginia & Maryland Coach Co. v. NLRB, 301 U.S. 142 (1937).

7. The last proviso refers to the rights of unions to insist that all workers within the unit become members of the union under a closed shop agreement, discussed infra. The relevant language in §8(a)(3) provides "That nothing in this Act, . . . shall preclude an employer from making an agreement with a labor organization to require as a condition of employment membership therein. . . ."

8. 73 Stat. 519 (1959) 29 U.S.C. §§ 401–531.

The NLRA was revolutionary in its implications for American labor law.[9] The two central pillars of the original NLRA have survived to this day. The first was a system of union democracy whereby unions could only obtain the rights of exclusive representation for firms if they could prevail in elections held by secret ballot. If a union was selected, both parties were under an obligation to negotiate in good faith to work toward a collective bargaining agreement. In addition, the legislative history of the NLRA went to great pains to establish a second pillar of free negotiation. In its own words,

> [t]he committee wishes to dispel any possible false impression that this bill is designed to compel the making of agreements or to permit governmental supervision of their terms. It must be stressed that the duty to bargain collectively does not carry with it the duty to reach an agreement because the essence of collective bargaining is that either party shall be free to decide whether proposals made to it are satisfactory.[10]

EFCA's Three Prongs

The Card Check

EFCA rejects both these fundamental commitments of the NLRA. Its defenders have attacked the current structure under the NLRA as inhospitable to unions.[11] The EFCA contains three provisions which, if enacted into law, would transform the institution of collective bargaining. The first proposal would allow the option to

9. *See* Calvert Magruder, A Half Century of Legal Influence Upon the Development of Collective Bargaining, 50 Harv. L. Rev. 1071 (1937).

10. S. Rep. No.573, 74th Cong. 1st Sess. (1935), reprinted in 2 Legislative History of the National Labor Relations Act of 1935, at 2312 (1985).

11. *See, e.g.,* Katherine V.W. Stone, *From Widgets to Digits: Employment Regulation for the Changing Workplace* (Cambridge University Press 2004); Cynthia Estlund, The Ossification of American Labor Law, 102 Colum. L. Rev. 1527 (2002); Paul Weiler, Promises to Keep: Security Workers' Rights to Self-Organization, 96 Harv. L. Rev. 1769 (1983).

substitute a card-check system for the current electoral system. To be sure, the EFCA leaves in place the present NLRA provisions that allow unions to proceed by filing a representation petition supported by thirty percent or more of employees in an appropriate bargaining unit and then holding elections.[12] Nonetheless, it seems clear that in virtually all cases the card check will displace the secret ballot. Virtually all major unions choose to file representation petitions only after they have accumulated signed authorization cards from well over fifty percent of unit members. They need that cushion because they know from experience that worker defections will take place during the course of any election campaign in which management can present its own case of the disadvantages of representation. No rational union would risk an election if it had authorization cards from just over fifty percent of the members of the unit it seeks to represent. As a practical matter, however, EFCA would displace union elections with the new card-check procedure. No union is likely to file for an election with more than thirty percent but less than fifty percent of signed authorization cards in the hope of improving its position during a campaign. The conversion to the card-check system is likely to prove well-nigh complete.

Compulsory Interest Arbitration

EFCA's second major provision would introduce a system of compulsory interest arbitration that leads to a first "contract" of two years duration. The term "contract" is put in quotation marks because an actual agreement that obtains the assent of both parties is not required during this initial period. This mandatory first contract, moreover, is not limited to wage matters, but must cover all

---

12. The current rules are set forth in NLRA § 9(c)(1) through (5) and § 9(e)(1) and (2), 29 U.S.C. § 159(e)(1) and (2), and simply adds a new Section 9(c)(6) and (7) to the Act. See Appendix.

the issues that are typically hammered out by agreement under the current system.

Increased Penalties for Employer Unfair Labor Practices

The third major change of the EFCA, which ties in closely with the adoption of the card-check system, substantially increases the penalties imposed on employers for violations of section 8(a)(3) of the NLRA, which prohibits discrimination against employees for union activities.[13] This section also requires the National Labor Relations Board to give priority to charges of unfair labor practices that arise in the course of organizing campaigns, in order to back-stop the advantage that unions expect to receive from the addition of the card-check alternative.

EFCA's Economic Consequences

If these provisions become law, they will radically alter the balance of power between management and labor. Their impact would extend to virtually all businesses, except for some small businesses that fall below the "interstate commerce" threshold of the NLRB.[14] But even those exemptions have little relevance to any new firm that hopes to grow over time. The bottom line, therefore, is that the passage of EFCA will create huge dislocations in established ways of doing business that will in turn lead to large losses in productivity. Small businesses, which count as the largest source of new jobs in the country, will find themselves besieged with insistent demands for unionization. These businesses often operate on small

---

13. It is an unfair labor practice for an employer "by discrimination in regard to hire or tenure or employment or any term or condition of employment to encourage or discourage membership in any labor organization. . . ."

14. *See generally* Robert A. Gorman & Matthew W. Finkin, *Basic Text on Labor Law, Unionization and Collective Bargaining* (West Publishing Co. 2004).

budgets, without the assistance of full-time lawyers. Under EFCA, their first exposure to unions could come at the conclusion of a secret campaign, which requires them to both hire and acquire expertise on contentious matters with which they are ill-equipped to deal, at a cost which they can ill afford to bear. These calls for unionization will divert management from the essential tasks of product development, marketing, and sales. EFCA will thus retard the formation of small businesses, as fledgling entrepreneurs reassess their prospects of success versus the danger of early derailment. In the long term, the EFCA will reduce business formation, depriving the economy of a central driver of new job creation and technology growth.

Large firms face a different set of difficulties. Like their smaller compatriots, they will face the heavy costs of meeting simultaneous multiple threats of unionization. Since they operate through geographically dispersed divisions, they face the risk of inconsistent arbitral decrees that will impede the development of firm-wide practices. Given the uncertain scope of these decrees, restrictions designed to preserve job security within a unit may limit the firm's ability to reorganize closely connected non-unit employees. The prospect of multiple union arbitrations covering different locations could result in inconsistent "first contracts" under a system that offers no clear avenues for appeal or clarification. Faced with these constraints, a firm's ability to meet rising competition from new firms could easily result in job losses as business lines fail, or the conscious redeployment by management of assets and new investment to locations with lower costs and greater flexibility—traits most often associated with nonunion operations. Sending more activities offshore is also a likely if unwelcome consequence. Any efforts to stem that flow could easily lead to a collapse of the entire firm in the face of effective foreign competition. Nonunionized firms are able to make these decisions in anticipation of a union threat. Firms bound by collective bargaining agreements of course remain subject to core obligations under the NLRA, including the duty to bargain in good faith, without any anti-union animus.[15] Unions may try to challenge some of these decisions before the NLRB, but the powerful rationales for taking these measures will reduce the chances of union success. Yet if the EFCA were in place, the level of labor tension and strife would be likely to increase the frequency and intensity of public protests, political campaigns, and work slowdowns or stoppages in response to decisions to relocate or outsource. The union leaders who link these key business decisions to "[t]he Senseless Slaughter of the Good American Job," tantamount to "wanton acts of physical violence,"[16] will not take kindly to lawful decisions to set up shop elsewhere. The same can be said of officials like SEIU President Andy Stern, who is intent on the restoration of the American dream and who is not likely to pull in his horns if EFCA does not meet his expectations. The next round of direct action and new legislative fixes offers the path of least resistance. Economic dislocation under EFCA will lead to further strife, not industrial peace.

Of course, the exact pattern of union threats, maneuvers, and responses is difficult to predict owing in part to the huge gaps in EFCA. But regardless of how these play out, it is certain that these devastating effects would arise chiefly from the synergistic effects of the first two provisions mentioned above. Taken together, they allow a union that acquires a sufficient number of signatures through a largely unregulated card-authorization process to force management to accept a first "contract"—in reality an arbitral

---

15. *See*, for discussion of the various obligations under Sections 8(a)(3) & 8(a)(5), see the discussion of Textile Workers Union v. Darlington Manufacturing Co. 380 U.S. 263 (1965).

16. *See*, John Sweeney, Address at the National Press Club, Washington, D.C., available at aflcio.org/mediacenter/prsptm/sp01182006.cfm. The full passage reads:

"We hear and read a lot about the violence in our cities, and the word most often used to describe it is 'senseless' — the death of a young man here in Washington, DC over New Year's was characterized in the media as 'senseless.'

It seems to me we should use the same language not just to describe wanton acts of physical violence, but also to depict the violence being visited upon working families and our communities by the killing of good jobs."

decree—that lasts for two years. Step one under the EFCA would displace the long-established system of union elections by routinely allowing any union that presents cards signed by a majority (e.g., 50 percent plus one) of the workers in an appropriate bargaining unit to become the bargaining agent for all the workers, including those who had no knowledge of the campaign from coworkers or the employer. For some workers, at least, the misnamed EFCA would leave them no choice at all if they were not approached during the campaign.

The EFCA's second provision introduces a system of "interest arbitration"—in reality compulsory arbitration—which takes effect if the two sides fail to reach an agreement within 130 days after union recognition. (This is a short time for any first-time collective bargaining agreement that starts with a blank sheet of paper.) The result is the appointment of a panel of arbitrators to impose by decree the first two-year contract. Under the proposed timetable, negotiations are supposed to begin within 10 days of union recognition. On the other hand, the union knows in advance the targets of its card-check drives and can have its negotiation team in place before the results of the card check are computed. The element of surprise gives the union a huge strategic advantage over a small business, which may not even be able to find a lawyer to represent it during this short initial period. Large firms suffer from the same tactical disadvantage. Yet even if they take the costly step of having some negotiation teams in place, they could still be besieged by multiple claims at the same time, which could leave them short on vital resources.

These difficulties are aggravated by the remainder of the statutory cycle. In the second stage the parties would have ninety days—a short time for addressing the multiplicity of issues in play—to reach a voluntary settlement. If an agreement were not reached by this time, then a mediator from the Federal Mediation and Conciliation Service (FMCS) would work with the parties for thirty days before the matter goes before a panel of arbitrators.

Once again, it is quite possible that just scheduling meetings for the relevant negotiators—all of whom are likely to have multiple commitments—could be difficult within the statutory period.

The entire time for negotiation could easily be consumed by collateral matters that quickly drive the case to arbitration, at which point it is anyone's guess what will happen. The EFCA provides no limitation on how long the arbitration panel may take to make its decision, and does not indicate what happens to the various open issues for the bargaining unit that were left unresolved during the interim period. Its basic procedures and powers are all to be determined by regulations under the statute, none of which will be drafted when the EFCA takes effect. Any effort to participate in the process whereby these regulations are drafted imposes additional costs, which are likely to prove especially large for small businesses that have no direct experience with the administrative process.

Why Unions Decline

Unions and their backers seek to justify this profound reversal of seventy unbroken years under the NLRA by claiming that radical surgery offers the only effective way to reverse the rapid decline in union membership in the private sector. It is of course undisputed that the level of private sector unionization has fallen from its high of about 35 percent of eligible workers in 1954 to about 8 percent of eligible workers today. Union supporters argue that this decline in unionization rates has had adverse consequences on the social fabric including the fragile status of the middle class. In her highly influential study on union elections, Professor Kate Bronfenbrenner of Cornell University, who herself has extensive experience as an organizer for the Service Employees International Union,[17] sounds the general theme by insisting that the overall increase in

---

17. *See* Bronfenbrenner's CV available at http://www.ilr.cornell.edu/directory/klb23/.

social prosperity in the 1990s did not translate into higher wages for workers. Indeed, she claims that her study "conclusively demonstrates that capital mobility and the threat of capital mobility have had a profound impact on the ability of American workers to exercise their rights to freedom of association and collective bargaining."[18] Her point illustrates a misunderstanding of the basic picture. What she should have said was that it is impossible for unions (and their domestic employers) to claim monopoly rents in the face of global competition, which is more powerful for businesses that can be moved offshore than for those service industries that remain at home. But it is not that the rights of association are stripped. It is that their value cannot be preserved against new entrants. What Bronfenbrenner does not acknowledge is that only the willingness of unions to back off their demands is what saves their jobs—when it is not too little, too late. Union intransigence would not stave off the demise of firm and union alike in the absence of tariff walls.

Nor is she correct in her claim that the market has left workers behind. The basic picture can be fleshed out by looking at data that examine the relationship in the broad economy between individual wages and individual productivity. The standard neoclassical economic theory on this point is confident in its prediction. Workers as a group in the general economy face a competitive labor market, in large measure because of the low levels of union penetration in the private sector. Accordingly, we should expect wages to be bid up to reflect any increase in productivity, for the possibility of switching jobs will force wages up. Just that result is found by looking at government statistics that seek to correlate these two key variables. The basic chart, as prepared by the conservative Heritage Foundation, shows an exceedingly close statistical correlation.

It is a mistake to think that the decline in labor union membership is unique to the United States. In fact, that change in the

---

18. *Id.* at v.

FIGURE 1

PRODUCTIVITY AND COMPENSATION GROWS, 1947–2007

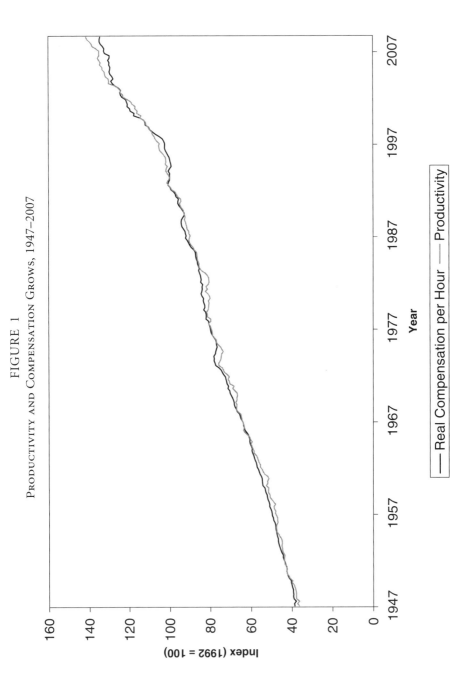

NOTE: Supra note 19, at 45. We added the relative changes calculations. Note that in some cases the absolute change does not match with the yearly data due to data availability.

United States is matched by the decline in unionization in other nations that operate under different legal regimes.[19] The extent of the decrease can be judged by looking at Table 1, which shows a uniform pattern of steep declines. In this regard, the New Zealand experience, although small in number, is of interest because the dramatic drop after 1990—from 51 percent in 1990 to 24.9 percent in 1996—was precipitated in part by the passage of the Employment Contract Act of 1991 initiated by the National, or conservative, party.[20] Yet when the Labour Party undid the earlier reforms by passing the Employment Relations Act—the change in terminology is no accident—upon taking power in 2000, the percentage of union participation barely budged. The key point that should be gathered from these figures is that any effort to attribute the decline in the American market to distinctive factors of our own system of labor law sorely misses the point. Larger, global trends are very much in evidence, which undercut the key union claim that distinctive American bargaining procedures drive the current decline in union membership.[21]

The key dispute is over the reasons for this indisputable decline. The defenders of EFCA typically claim that unions suffer a serious disadvantage in an organizing campaign because the unjustified intransigence of employers both large and small, including the use of unfair labor practices, prevents workers from exercising free choice to join a union—the equal right to refrain from joining a union receives less attention—contained in the essential guarantee for collective bargaining after the 1947 Taft-Hartley amendments to the NLRA.

---

19. Jelle Visser, Union Membership Statistics in 24 Countries, 129 Monthly Lab. Rev. 38 (January 2006).

20. For discussion, see Richard A. Epstein, Employment and Labor Law Reform in New Zealand, 33 Case W. Res. J. Int'l L. 361 (2001).

21. Samuel Estreicher, "Think Global, Act Local" Employee Representation in a World of Global Labor and Product Market Competition, New York University Public Law and Legal Theory Working Papers No. 90, (2008) available at http://lsr.nellco.org/cgi/viewcontent.cgi?article = 1090&context; eqnyu/plltwp.

TABLE 1
UNION DENSITY IN 11 COUNTRIES AND E. U., ADJUSTED DATA, 1970–2003, IN %

Year	United States	Canada	Australia	New Zealand	Japan	Rep. of Korea	Euro. Union	Germany	France	Italy	U. K.	Ireland
1970	23.5	31.6	50.2	55.2	35.1	12.6	37.8	32.0	21.7	37.0	44.8	53.2
1980	19.5	34.7	49.5	69.1	31.1	14.7	39.7	34.9	18.3	49.6	50.7	57.1
1990	15.5	32.9	40.5	51.0	25.4	17.6	33.1	31.2	10.1	38.8	39.3	51.1
1991	15.5	—	—	44.4	24.8	16.1	34.1	36.0	9.9	38.7	38.5	50.2
1992	15.1	33.1	39.6	37.1	24.5	15.1	33.4	33.9	9.9	38.9	37.2	49.8
1993	15.1	32.8	37.6	34.5	24.3	14.5	32.7	31.8	9.6	39.2	36.1	47.7
1994	14.9	—	35.0	30.2	24.3	13.4	31.7	30.4	9.2	38.7	34.2	46.2
1995	14.3	—	32.7	27.6	24.0	12.9	30.4	29.2	9.0	38.1	32.6	45.8
1996	14.0	—	31.1	24.9	23.4	12.2	29.5	27.8	8.3	37.4	31.7	45.5
1997	13.6	28.8	30.3	23.6	22.8	11.9	28.8	27.0	8.2	36.2	30.6	43.5
1998	13.4	28.5	28.1	22.3	22.5	12.1	28.2	25.9	8.0	35.7	30.1	41.5
1999	13.4	27.9	25.7	21.9	22.2	11.1	27.8	25.6	8.1	36.1	29.8	—
2000	12.8	28.1	24.7	22.7	21.5	11.1	27.3	25.0	8.2	34.9	29.7	—
2001	12.8	28.2	24.5	22.6	20.9	11.2	26.6	23.5	8.1	34.8	29.3	36.6
2002	12.6	28.2	23.1	22.1	20.3	11.1	26.3	23.2	8.3	34.0	29.2	36.3
2003	12.4	28.4	22.9	—	19.7	11.2	—	22.6	8.3	33.7	29.3	35.3
Absolute Change												
1970–1980	−2.5	3.3	−0.7	13.9	−4.0	2.0	1.9	2.9	−3.4	12.6	5.9	3.9
1980–1990	−4.0	−1.8	−9.0	−18.1	−5.8	3.0	−6.7	−3.7	−8.1	−10.8	−11.4	−6.1
1990–2003	−3.1	−4.7	−17.6	−28.9	−5.6	−6.5	−6.7	−8.6	−1.9	−5.1	−10.0	−15.8
1970–2003	−11.1	−6.5	−27.3	−33.1	−15.4	−1.5	−11.5	−9.5	−13.4	−3.3	−15.5	−17.9
Relative Change												
1970–1980	−10.6	10.4	−1.4	25.2	−11.4	15.9	5.0	9.1	−15.7	34.1	13.2	7.3
1980–1990	−20.5	−5.2	−18.2	−26.2	−18.6	20.4	−16.9	−10.6	−44.3	−21.8	−22.5	−10.7
1990–2003	−20.0	−14.3	−43.5	−56.7	−22.0	−36.9	−20.2	−27.6	−18.8	−13.1	−25.4	−30.9
1970–2003	−47.2	−20.6	−54.4	−60.0	−43.9	−11.9	−30.4	−29.7	−61.8	−8.9	−34.6	−33.6

NOTE: Supra note 19, at 45. We added the relative changes calculations. Note that in some cases the absolute change does not match with the yearly

FIGURE 2
U.S. UNION DENSITY, 1977–2007

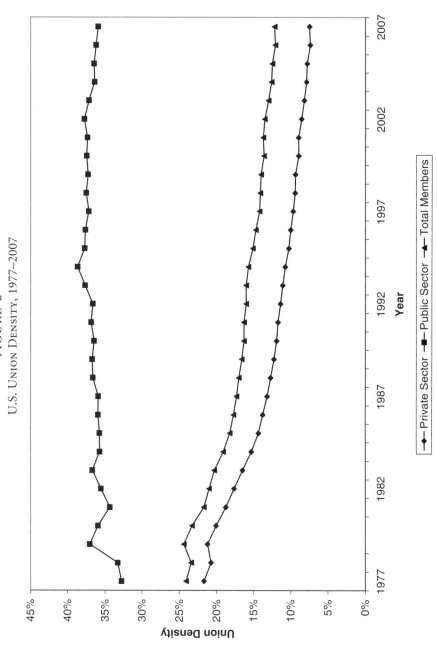

—◆— Private Sector —■— Public Sector —▲— Total Members

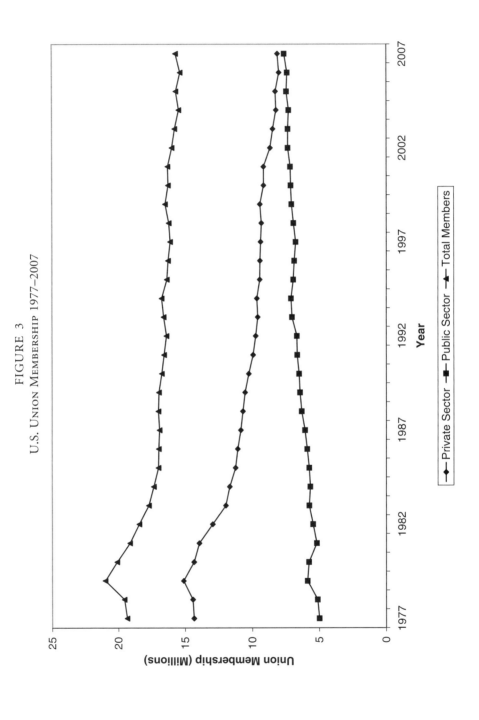

FIGURE 3

U.S. Union Membership 1977–2007

FIGURE 4

U.S. UNION MEMBERSHIP RELATIVE TO NONUNION MEMBERSHIP 1977–2007

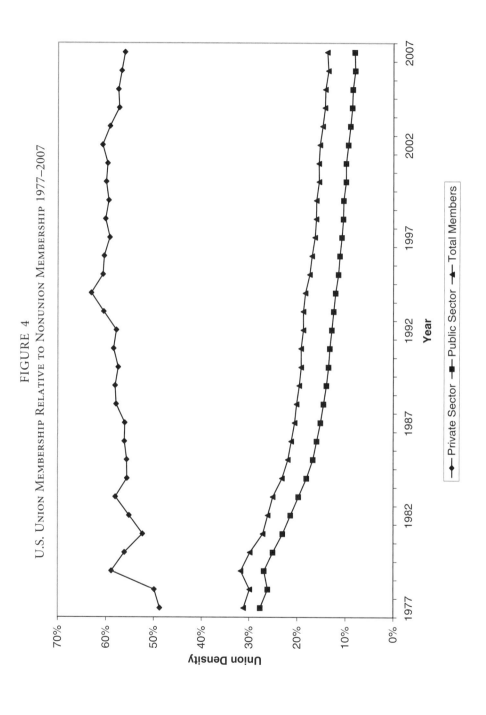

Union Density

Year

Private Sector — Public Sector — Total Members

In making this claim, the critics of the current law ignore not only the global trends noted above, but all other factors that could account for the decline in unionization. Some likely reasons include the expansion of free trade across national borders, more intensive global competition for employees, the reduced appeal of unions to younger workers,[22] the entry of smaller decentralized firms, the rapid turnover of workers in a relatively open economy, the better wages and working conditions that nonunion employees can command in an open economy, the rise in government regulations that confer certain protections (i.e., against discrimination) that no longer are subjects of bargaining, ineffective union organizing, and the rigidity of the internal governance structure of unions themselves. Most important perhaps is the fundamental switch in the political economy of the United States. The 1930s marked a corporatist period, in which monopoly unions shared power with regulated monopoly industries, shielded from competition by a powerful state.[23] More recently, the economic environment has switched by allowing the free entry of smaller firms whose vitality and growth have gone a long way toward undermining the old monopoly models, posing more challenges to established firms and their longstanding labor unions. No account of the decline in unionization is complete without taking these changes into consideration, which the defenders of EFCA refuse to do.

The case in support of EFCA is also deficient for its failure to establish any tight relationship between the supposed wrong and the curative legislation. Of EFCA's three provisions, the only one that deals directly with the incidence of unfair labor practices is the third, which imposes increased penalties on employers without,

---

22. It is striking that the percentage of union workers in the workforce is higher in older groups than in younger ones. Thus workers under 35 are less likely to be union members than older workers. Part of this shift may be attributable to their want of opportunity to join a union. But part of it is a shift in attitudes that may remain as these workers get older.

23. *See*, for discussion, Michael Wachter, Labor Unions: A Corporatist Institution in a Competitive World, 155 U. Pa. L. Rev. 581 (2007).

however, imposing a similar increase on unions for any ULPs *they* might commit. In other words, the EFCA does not contain any parallel provision that imposes increased penalties on unions with respect to their violation of the analogous ULPs contained in NLRA section 8(b)(1)(A), which prohibits union restraint or coercion of employees; section 8(b)(3), which imposes on unions the obligation to bargain in good faith during negotiations; and section 8(b)(4), which prohibits unlawful union pressure directed against secondary parties in order to improperly place pressure on the employer engaged in union bargaining. EFCA only increases the penalties for employers.

The proposal for the standard substitution of a card-check system for the secret ballot is overly broad because it imposes this new method of union recognition in all cases, based on the occurrence of ULPs in some small fraction of cases, which is systematically overstated by union defenders. The insistence on interest arbitration—a fancy phrase for compulsory labor arbitration—is described misleadingly in the bill as a means of "facilitating initial collective bargaining agreements," when in fact unions are frustrated by their inability to obtain first contracts that advance their interests under the traditional bargaining system. Federal and state laws have never allowed any panel of arbitrators to impose a full array of detailed obligations on a reluctant party. In fact, the NLRA's definition of collective bargaining explicitly states that the law does not require either party to accept a particular proposal or to make a particular concession (NLRA § 8(d), 29 U.S.C. § 158(d)). Without question, this dramatic switch in the current law enjoys no precedent in the private sector and, as will become evident, only highly imperfect analogies in the public sector.

All the public defenses of the EFCA, including the testimony before Congress on March 27, 2007, skirt the interest arbitration question entirely. Professor Cynthia Estlund of the New York University School of Law, for example, ducked the arbitration issue with the simple observation that she was concerned only with "enhanced enforcement and majority sign-up process," without ever explaining why it was appropriate to ignore the evident synergies between the two.[24] None of the other parties who testified addressed it either. It is as though a conspiracy of silence among EFCA supporters envelops the one provision that most dramatically transforms the American system of collective bargaining for the worse.

In this extended essay, I hope to fill the large gaps that previous advocacy and research leave open in understanding EFCA. My approach proceeds in two stages. The first parses the card-check and arbitration provisions of the EFCA. The second offers a detailed critique of its institutional structure and probable economic consequences on allocative and distributional grounds.[25]

---

24. Strengthening America's Middle Class Through the Employee Free Choice Act Hearing on S.1041 Before the Senate Comm. on Health, Education, Labor and Pensions, note 8 (2007) (statement of Cynthia Estlund, Catherine A. Rein Professor of Law, NYU School of Law) available at http://help.senate.gov/Hearings/2007_03_27_a/Estlund.pdf.

25. For my views on the current labor law regime, see Richard A. Epstein, A Common Law for Labor Relations: A Critique of the New Deal Legislation, 92 Yale L.J. 1357 (1983); Richard A. Epstein, In Defense of the Contract at Will, 51 U. Chi. L. Rev. 947 (1984).

CHAPTER 1
CARD CHECKS VERSUS SECRET BALLOT ELECTIONS

STREAMLINING UNION CERTIFICATION?

Section 2 of the Employee Free Choice Act is described as "Streamlining Union Certification." That heading connotes an effort to fine-tune the current system in order to make it work more cheaply, quickly, and effectively. But this title belies the major changes that the section imposes, which would gut the entire system of union elections. The power of the union is, of course, inversely proportional to the ability of the employer to influence the outcome of the election. By increasing penalties for employer, but not union, ULPs, section 4 of the EFCA, "Strengthening Enforcement," tilts the scale in unions' favor, without any effective mechanism for remedying abuses associated with union authorization cards or petitions. These two provisions significantly alter all aspects of any union organization drive. In this chapter I compare current law position under the NLRA with the proposed change. My examination of the process leading to union certification or rejection begins with the preliminary efforts unions make to secure an advantageous outcome either through an election or card check under current law. In particular, I examine neutrality agreements and the issue of salted employees. I next turn to the conduct of an election campaign and a comparison of the secret ballot and the card check. Charges and countercharges of coercion and intimidation are thrown about with great abandon, and must be examined at every stage.

A Fatal Imbalance?

The bedrock issue is this: do the current rules contain some implicit bias against union organization? In order to assess this charge, it is necessary to look at all three phases of these elections: preliminary maneuvers, the actual election campaign, and the conduct of the election itself. In making this assessment, a note of diffidence is needed. The peculiar circumstances of union elections cannot be governed by rules that carry over from the political context without some adaptation to the distinctive context of worker elections under the NLRA. But it hardly follows from this proposition that NLRA union-representation elections are tainted when measured against some benchmark of political elections. Both types of election are, and must remain, flawed under any test that requires election outcomes to be a perfect reflection of voter preferences. The only workable questions ask what fixes could be made to improve the situation with respect to either the campaign or the election itself.

The source of this cautious assessment lies in large measure in one constant feature of all electoral contexts—the built-in *asymmetry* among the contending parties. In a political election, one asymmetry arises whenever one party is able to reap the advantages of incumbency, which allow its candidates to reach voters through legitimate government expenditures that lie outside campaign finance limitations.[1]

---

1. For a discussion of these issues, *see* McConnell v. Federal Election Commission, 540 U.S. 93 (2003), where the issue is raised in the opinions of Justices Breyer, Kennedy and Scalia; see also McIntyre v. Ohio Elections Comm'n, 514 U.S. 334 (1995); Buckley v. Valeo, 424 U.S. 1 (1976); FEC v. Public Citizen, 268 F.3d 1283 (2001). For a discussion of the

The constant efforts of government regulators to create fund-raising or spending limits that cancel out these advantages necessarily fall short. Yet the Supreme Court has properly taken pains to indicate that the level of scrutiny given to these reforms cannot be so high as to preclude all forms of government regulation, even if incumbents keep their insider advantage against challengers.

The challenge to devise appropriate electoral safeguards is not confined to cases where one party is the incumbent. Various strategic imbalances also arise when two or more candidates vie for an office with no incumbent. In the 2004 presidential election, the contribution of the so-called 527 organizations, including the Swift Vets and POWs for Truth, had a powerful negative impact on the fortunes of John Kerry.[2] And the decision of Barack Obama to forgo public money in the 2008 campaign generated a huge media advantage that manifested itself most clearly in the closing days of the election. More generally, massive contributions from political action committees organized by activist groups, including labor unions, can exert a profound effect on electoral outcomes. In the recent election, unions contributed $450 million to elect Democratic candidates, $85 million of which was contributed by the Service Employees International Union.[3] The most candid appraisal about the purpose of these contributions comes from SEIU's Andy Stern, who was not just worried about who gets elected. Quite consciously, he said, SEIU put aside "an additional $10 million to get people unelected if need be." Stern explained, "We would like to make sure people appreciate that we take them at their word and when they don't live up to their word there should be consequences."[4]

---

problem, see Richard Hasen, Buckley is Dead: Long Live Buckley: The New Campaign Finance Incoherence of McConnell v. Federal Election Commission, 153 U. Penn. L. Rev. 31, (2004).

2. *See* Wikipedia, Swiftboating, http://en.wikipedia.org/wiki/Swiftboat.
3. *See* Matthew Kaminski, Let's Share the Wealth, Wall St. J., Dec. 6, 2008, at A9.
4. *Id.*

Quite simply, it is impossible to devise election rules that do not create advantages for one side or the other. In the course of any complex campaign, advantages run in both directions, from which it does *not* follow that any two sets of advantages necessarily cancel each other out. The same basic insight carries over to union elections, where the asymmetries are guaranteed by the fundamental difference in the position of the two major parties, and the closed environment in which campaigns take place. It is important to review the evidence to see the extent to which any charge of systematic unfairness accounts for the decline in union participation. The overall answer is that it is difficult to postulate any large employer advantage. Indeed, with the increase of collateral attacks that unions make on employers outside and prior to the election process, the organizing advantage has tilted in their favor. There is no evidence of any systematic shift in the rules governing campaigns or elections. Nor is there any evidence of administrative bias in the conduct of elections at the NLRB in either direction.

The Organization Campaign

Neutrality Agreements

The current union antipathy toward recognition elections has led union leaders to seek aggressively so-called neutrality agreements to negate what they regard as the inherently coercive nature of union elections.[5] They defend these agreements as a way to counter the various tactics that employers reportedly use to resist unionization, including captive meetings, e-mail blasts, and supervisor persuasion

---

5. For one such defense, see James J. Brudney, Neutrality Agreements and Card Check Recognition: Prospects for Changing Paradigms, 90 Iowa L. Rev. 819 (2005); and in shorter form James J. Brudney, Neutrality Agreements and Card Check Recognition: Prospects for Changing Labor Relations Paradigms, available at http://www.acslaw.org/files/Brudney -Neutrality%20Agreements-Feb%2 02007-Advance %20Vol%201.pdf.

which, according to EFCA proponents, pummel workers into voting against the union.[6]

The terms of neutrality agreements vary from case to case, but the basic pattern in about two-thirds of the cases is that the employer agrees to waive the right to a representation election and to accept the outcome of a card-check campaign organized by the union.[7] In the remainder of the agreements, some limitations on employer speech, from modest to severe, are accepted, but the card-check provision is rejected. Not all of these agreements require the union to agree to any similar restraints, but some do. These agreements have an uneasy status because they do not necessarily reflect the interests of employees who care about the election or about the opportunity to hear the other side. Many of these agreements are made in secret between unions and large employers. An example is the secret engagement involving Sodexho Inc. and Compass Group USA with the SEIU and Unite Here.[8] The parties claimed that they needed secrecy for competitive reasons, and this may well have worked to the advantage of both sides, given the range of pressures that unions can bring against employers.

This claim should be greeted with suspicion. As a matter of general contract law, agreements that bind third parties without their consent are highly suspect, and these neutrality agreements as a class are not exempt from that criticism. Section 7 of the NLRA protects the rights of neither unions nor employers, but of employees—all employees. The goal is not to protect unionization as such.

6. Kate L. Bronfenbrenner, Employer Behavior in Certification Elections and First-Contract Campaigns: Implications for Labor Law Reform, in *Restoring the Promise of American Labor Law 75* (Sheldon Friedman et al. eds. 1994); William T. Dickens, The Effect of Company Campaigns on Certification Elections: Law & Reality Once Again, 36 Industrial & Lab. Rev. 560 (1983); Richard B. Freeman & Morris M. Kleiner, Employer Behavior in the Face of Union Organizing Drives, 43 Indus. & Lab. Rel. Rev. 351 (1990); Morris M. Kleiner, Intensity of Management Resistance: Understanding the Decline of Unionization in the Private Sector, 22 J. Lab. Res. 519 (2001)

7. *See* Adrienne E. Eaton & Jill Kriesky, Union Organizing Under Neutrality and Card Check Agreements, 55 Indus. & Lab. Rel. Rev. 42, 45 (2001).

8. Kris Maher, Unions Forge Secret Pacts with Major Employers, Wall St. J., May 10, 2006 at A1.

Rather, current law accepts the ability of employees to set up unions through card checks, but prefers union elections.[9]

It is easy to see why labor unions would support card-check procedures. They improve the union's chances of gaining recognition,[10] even if they limit the voices and remove the votes of dissenting workers. It is, of course, harder to see why employers who are opposed to unions would be willing to accept these provisions. In many cases, neutrality agreements result from persistent "corporate campaigns" waged by unions against employers, either in the absence of any bargaining relationship or where the union represents employees at some, but not all, company facilities. In these cases, paradoxically, it is often in the interest of unions to *postpone* the election in order to continue their pressure on the firm. Yet the current interpretation of the NLRA does not give the employer the option to force an election unless the union has clearly announced its willingness to go ahead with it.[11] In other cases, the employer's decision may be simply bowing to the inevitable, a rational calculation to avoid greater loss. If a union is known to be in a strong position, the neutrality agreement spares the firm the costs of contesting an election while holding out some small hope that the union will not be able to gain a sufficient number of cards to force recognition or to win an election if one is still allowed. So the outcome could be chalked up to simple economic rationality.

Neutrality agreements do not always have the benevolent origins

---

9. *See* NLRB v. Gissel Packing Co., 395 U.S. 575, 595–600 (1969).

10. Some evidence from Canadian card check points to an increase in union certification rates by a switch from elections to card checks of around 9 percent, see Susan Johnson, Card Check or Mandatory Representation Vote? How the Type of Union Recognition Procedure Affects Union Certification Success, 112 Econ J. 344, 356 (2002). See also, Chris Riddell, Union Certification Success under Voting Versus Card-Check Procedures: Evidence from British Columbia, 1978–1998, 57 INDUS. & LAB. REL. REV. 493 (2004), reporting a 19 percent decrease in certification when the card check was removed in British Columbia, which was followed an increase in the same amount when it was reinstated.

11. *See, e.g.,* MGM Grand, 329 NLRB, 464, 469 (1999), where the dissent of Member Brame notes that the union "vigorously" sought to organize the MGM Grand, but never sought an election, preferring to gain employer consent to a card check.

their supporters claim. Professor James Brudney, for example, points to other collateral advantages that unions can dangle before management in order to get it to sign neutrality agreements, including steering access to union conventions to hotels that accept these agreements.[12] Unfortunately, when the carrot does not work, the stick is still available. There is enormous variation in the regulatory environment of firms covered by the NLRA. Employers, in some industries at least, are vulnerable to union pressure on other fronts. That point has not escaped Stern, the most dynamic leader in the labor movement, who put the point forward with frightening bluntness: "We like to say: We use the power of persuasion first. If it doesn't work, we try the persuasion of power."[13] Stern may have no formal training in game theory, but he has an instinctive grasp of its central principles. The person who hears the initial persuasive pitch knows what to expect if he does not agree: a switch into second gear. The maxim shows that SEIU will not need to expend unnecessary labor so long as its second-stage threat is credible.

And it is. For example, SEIU has taken an active role as a vehement critic of all private equity firms. It recently urged the California Public Employees' Retirement System (CalPERS) against investing in certain companies that failed to meet labor standards acceptable to SEIU.[14] Stern has also mounted an extensive political campaign that targets private equity firms, most notably Kohlberg Kravis Roberts & Co. and The Carlyle Group, which have resisted unionization efforts by SEIU, by portraying them as "buyout monsters" whose greed threatens the health and stability of the middle class.[15] Clearly, these pressure tactics represent efforts to circumvent

12. *See* Convention Center Board Seeks Neutrality from San Diego Hotel Developers, Owners, Daily, Lab. Rep. (BNA), May 15, 2000, at A-8, cited in Brudney, Neutrality (II) at 16, note 2.

13. Kaminski, supra note 3.

14. Environmental standards are included in SEIU's guidelines as well. See Editorial, California's Stern Rebuke, Wall St. J., Apr. 21, 2008, at A16, and the response, Stephen Lerner, SEIU Seeks Ethics, Good Returns, Wall St. J., Apr. 26, 2008, at A8.

15. *See* Editorial, Andy Stern's Pensions, Wall St. J., Jul. 16, 2008, at A16.

unit elections by engaging in conduct that verges on, or crosses the line of, defamation, knowing that lawsuits on this matter are either doomed to fail or only give the targeted firm another dose of unwanted publicity. Such tough organizing tactics have the great advantage that retaliation in kind is impossible. There is nothing that Kohlberg Kravis Roberts or The Carlyle Group could say about SEIU's Stern that has one-thousandth of the pop of the bitter denunciations that he can make against them.

The SEIU campaigns, moreover, are not limited to pressures against particular unions, but also cover efforts to force business groups to back off their opposition to EFCA itself. In February 2009, Anna Burger wrote a public letter to the Financial Services Roundtable urging it to back off from its opposition to EFCA and to expel any member companies that received Troubled Asset Relief Program (TARP) funds and that opposed the legislation. Copies of the letter were pointedly sent to the key Democratic members of Congress most intimately connected with the endless bailout nego-tiations, Representative Barney Frank of Massachusetts and Senator Chris Dodd of Connecticut. Burger wrote, "At a time when the industry must devote every effort to economic recovery, it is shameful that the Financial Services Roundtable makes lobbying against the right of workers to organize a legislative priority and, worse yet, is using taxpayer-financed TARP subsidies to do so."[16] Ms. Burger is the international secretary-treasurer of SEIU, chair-woman of Change to Win, a labor coalition, and, most recently, a member of the President's Economic Recovery Advisory Board.[17] Her words therefore carry much institutional weight, so that we

---

16. Kevin Bogardus, Unions Warn Wall Street to Back Off, February 11, 2009, at Demo-cratic Underground.com, The Hill.com, http://www.democraticunderground.com/discuss/duboard.php?az = view_all&addre ss = 389x5035460.

17. See SEIU Blog, Anna Burger Named to President's Economic Recovery Advisory Board, February 6, 2009, http://www.seiu.org/2009/02/anna-burger-named-to-presidents-economic-recovery-advisory-board.php. The Board is "charged with offering independent, nonpartisan information, analysis, and advice to the President as he formulates and imple-ments his plans for economic recovery." Oh!

should ponder the implications of this position. There are strong reasons to think that EFCA will have precisely the opposite effect of what its backers claim; it will shrink labor markets in both new and existing businesses. So what about an effort to expel from business or labor groups anyone who supports EFCA if they hope to receive TARP funds? The effort to use political muscle to redirect TARP funds takes a program that is already suffering from a lack of focus and direction and turns it into a political football, by invoking a strategy of exclusion that anyone can play. The effort to use selective funding to shape political debate is, moreover, just the type of viewpoint discrimination in the distribution of public funds that is routinely struck down as unconstitutional, on the ground that it represents a government effort to skew the political debate.[18] If Congress could not vote TARP funds only to firms that contribute to the Democratic Party, it cannot direct them to firms that support deeply controversial positions.

Nor does the use of coercion—taken here in a narrow sense— stop with publicity campaigns. Litigation on collateral matters offers additional avenues through which to attack employers. One common union strategy is to file all sorts of lawsuits against employers for alleged violations of various labor statutes, the Fair Labor Standards Act, antidiscrimination laws, antitrust laws, and so forth in order to gain recognition as the bargaining agent or to obtain a neutrality agreement.[19] Here again the complaints are costly to respond to even if their charges are unmerited. These lawsuits at least are expensive to file and they require the identification of real plaintiffs, which anonymous complaints do not.

---

18. For a discussion of the doctrine of unconstitutional conditions in connection with freedom of speech, see Speiser v. Randall, 357 U.S. 513 (1958), striking down property tax exemptions given only to veterans that signed loyalty oaths. For a general account of the constitutional dangers of selective dispensation from government obligations, see Richard A. Epstein, Bargaining with the State 240–246 (1993).

19. See Ben Sachs, Employment Law as Labor Law 29 Cardozo L. Rev. 2685 (2008) (detailing how indirect campaigns were based on the Fair Labor Standards Act of 1938 and the Civil Rights Act of 1964). Sachs brackets the normative question of whether collective bargaining works. Id at 2692–93.

A still more potent technique takes advantage of the cumbrous machinery of the administrative state. The employers regulated by the NLRA are a diverse lot. Some of them work in highly unregulated industries, where regulatory retaliation and threats are difficult to launch. But other businesses are far more vulnerable. Hospitals for obvious reasons are among the most heavily regulated industries of all. Many of these regulatory groups will conduct on-the-spot inspections in response to anonymous tips and complaints. It is not difficult for unions—especially SEIU—to lodge multiple regulatory complaints in order to impose on an employer the heavy costs of dealing with the disruption caused by these inspections, which can damage patient care and public confidence.[20] The costs of bad publicity and compliance efforts are high even if, as is commonly the case, the complaints are eventually dismissed as groundless. On the other hand, the risk of liability or bad publicity to SEIU is negligible.

The increased reliance on these tactics is revealing in a more ominous sense. They indicate that SEIU and other unions do not think that they can persuade firms that they are better off with the unions than they are without them. These tactics are designed to alter the terms of trade. Now the SEIU strategy is to demonstrate to employers that they are better off with the union than they are suffering under the various tactics SEIU can impose unilaterally to undermine their ordinary operations. The social welfare implications of this alternative approach are profound. The voluntary acceptance of a union (especially in the absence of any duty to bargain) should in theory be treated as welfare-enhancing. When parties enter into ordinary business contracts it is strong evidence that they regard themselves as better off than before: why else go through the trouble? Acquiescence to a union in the face of these

---

20. For a defense of the aggressive posture see Andy Stern, *Getting America Back on Track: A Country that Works*, 59 (Free Press 2006). See also, Steven Findlay, Union: care compromised at Columbia Sunrise, Cloud of suspicion darkens troubled chain's hospital, USA Today, Sept. 22, 1997, at 8B.

constant threats only shows that the firm is better off with the union than with the threats that induced it to cave in. It does not show that the union can improve the level of production of the firm so as to make the firm (or society) better off with the union than without it. Nor is there any reason to think that efforts to placate an aggressive union do anything to improve the welfare of the firm's workers.

The use of these tactics by unions is a conscious effort to avoid the pitfalls of secret ballot elections, whose use has declined in recent years by close to 50 percent, from 2,705 in 2000 to 1,407 in 2007. Set against this background, an employer's decision to enter into a neutrality agreement in order to stave off a barrage of regulatory complaints hardly counts as voluntary. Instead, it is a rational calculation to avoid a greater peril that has nothing to do with the welfare of bargaining unit members. Section 8(b)(2) is not applicable because there is no "company" union. Pigeon-holing this conduct under section 8(b)(1)—which deals with the ULPs of labor organizations—is not as easy as it seems, for the section only applies to conduct "(1) to restrain or coerce (A) employees in the exercise of their rights guaranteed in section 7." The direct target of these initiatives is the employer, not the workers, so that the

TABLE 2
NUMBER OF NLRB ELECTIONS HELD 2000–2007

Year	Number of Elections
2000	2705
2001	2334
2002	2167
2003	2133
2004	1917
2005	2007
2006	1546
2007	1407

NOTE: Figures based on NLRB Election reports available at http://www.nlrb.gov/Publications/reports/election_reports.aspx. For a more detailed breakup see Table 3 infra, at 54.

section could only apply if the indirect effect on workers' rights were sufficient to trigger the application of the section, which presents a tricky point of statutory construction. But the abuse of false publicity and legal process, especially the latter, is apparent given that charges and complaints are often made without regard to the truth. One important labor reform would be to expand the scope of ULPs to cover these behaviors. When the question of reforms comes up, the legislative control of collateral attacks on employers and other employees should be part of the agenda, not something that is swept under the rug.

Salted Employees

Union efforts to combine economic leverage with administrative challenges and collateral litigation are matched with yet another tactic: the conscious exploitation of the NLRB's administrative processes. One approach involves the use of "salted" employees to test for unfair labor practices. Union members apply for jobs solely to set up potential violations of section 8(a)(3)[21]. The Supreme Court has construed that section to protect ordinary job applicants, even though they do not fall precisely within the statutory definition, which covers workers who have been let go, but not those who were never hired.[22] But salted "employees" do not deserve NLRB protection under this extended definition, for they frequently have no intention to accept any job offer. When they do take jobs, they have no commitment to the firm. Instead they frequently follow scripted union protocols that could drive nonunion firms from the market by overwhelming them with litigation costs, attorneys' fees,

---

21. The standard definition of salting refers to "the act of a trade union in sending a union member or members to an unorganized jobsite to obtain employment and then organize the employees." Tualatin Electric, 312 NLRB 129, 130 fn. 3 (1993), enfd. 84 F.3d 1202, 1203 fn. 1 (9th Cir. 1996).

22. *See* Phelps Dodge Corp. v. NLRB, 313 U.S. 177, 185–86 (1941)

and alleged back pay liability . . .[23] unless, of course, they accept union representation as the lesser evil.

For example, in *Toering Electrical*[24] the International Brotherhood of Electrical Workers applied its own manual by instructing a "salted" unionized electrical worker to provoke the confrontation that led to his dismissal. The worker promptly filed a claim that the employer had discriminated against union members under section 8(a)(3). A highly polarized board, by a three (Republican) to two (Democrat) majority, denied the claim, insisting that the Board "does not serve its intended statutory role as a neutral arbiter of disputes if it must litigate hiring discrimination charges filed on behalf of disingenuous applicants who intend no service and loyalty to a common enterprise with a targeted employer."[25]

The NLRB majority was right to clamp down on the practice. There is no shortage of bona fide job applicants who are in a position to test for an employer's anti-union animus. The absence of any independent claims offers good evidence that the employer has not violated its statutory obligation. Union testers are not neutral, so the risk of finding false positive ULPs is great. That problem is acute in dual motive cases where, as in *Toering Electrical*, the employer claims that outdated resumes and its ability to tap other available workers were the independent grounds that drove its decision. In these joint motivation cases, the employer must prove that the particular workers would not have been hired even if there had been no anti-union animus.[26] Union members therefore can rely on this favorable presumption to set up their ULP claims, by consciously acting in a blustery fashion while asserting pro-union sentiments, thereby forcing the employer to show that the bluster alone

---

23. Must Construction Take Its Hires With 'Salting' or Without?; Supreme Court to Decide Long-Standing Dispute Over Union Organizing Campaign at Town & Country Electric, Wash. Post, Apr.16, 1995, at H5.
24. 351 NLRB No. 18 (2007) at *3.
25. Id. at *32.
26. *See* for the shift in burdens in these joint motivation cases, NLRB v. Transportation Management Corp. 463 U.S. 393 (1983).

would have led to the discharge. Using testers is always dangerous business when the investigator has a vested interest in the outcome.[27] Given the total lack of any institutional safeguards against abuse, salting itself should be treated as a union ULP under section 8(b)(2) "to cause or attempt to cause an employer to discriminate against an employee in violation of subsection [8](a)(3)."

Free versus Coercive Speech

One of the most contentious claims by EFCA supporters is that the current process is heavily biased against them because of the employer's use of coercive tactics throughout the union organization campaign. A related but sensitive question that union supporters usually prefer to avoid is: Why do so many employers, both large and small, exhibit outward hostility or stony indifference toward a union during an organizing campaign? The simplest explanation is that they perceive that they have much to lose through unionization in the form of greater wage increases, more generous pension and health plans, restrictive work rules, work stoppages, and a general loss of management prerogatives. On these issues, they should be regarded as better judges of their own self-interest than the unions seeking recognition under the NLRA.

Yet in the face of this brutal economic reality, the implicit union premise is that an employer behaves improperly during an election by making known its preferences, even when there is nothing illegal about the presentation of its views. That extreme claim is unsupportable, especially in light of the explicit statutory framework used to regulate employer speech under section 8(c), which provides:

(c) **Expression of views without threat of reprisal or force or promise of benefit.** The expressing of any views, argument, or opinion, or the dissemination thereof, whether in written, printed,

27. *See, e.g.,* Ian Ayres, Fair Driving: Gender and Race Discrimination in Retail Car Negotiations, 104 Harv. L. Rev. 817 (1991); Ian Ayres, Further Evidence of Discrimination in New Car Negotiations and Estimates of Its Cause, 94 Mich. L. Rev. 109 (1995).

graphic, or visual form, shall not constitute or be evidence of an unfair labor practice under any of the provisions of this Act [sub-chapter], if such expression contains no threat of reprisal or force or promise of benefit.

The reason for this complex provision derives from the NLRA's complex structure that creates a bilateral monopoly under which any particular employer must negotiate with a particular union. Good-faith bargaining is so difficult because the monopolistic structures of collective bargaining insure that there is never a unique wage or set of conditions governing management-labor contracts. Unlike the position that parties find themselves in with competitive markets, there is always a wide range acceptable to both sides. Within that range each seeks to gain the best deal possible for itself. The exact distribution of gains and losses is impossible to predict in advance. Accordingly, the rules fashioned under the NLRA have had to take immense care to make sure that neither side obtains too dominant a bargaining position.

Section 8(c) represents an effort to work out a delicate compromise about employer speech that is most vital when it matters the most—in the context of union elections. Employer speech provides valuable information to workers. Workers need to be able to form an educated view on the long-term implications of union representation, which includes some estimate as to how well employees think the union and employer will work together. Employees can form that judgment only by collecting information from all sides. The relevant information includes some sense of the employer's reaction to the initial contract negotiations, ongoing informal adjustments, and future contracts. None of that information is available if employers lack an appropriate forum in which to voice their own views. In all other walks of life, individuals are allowed to make clear their response, positive or negative, to participating with others in proposed business deals. In most business contexts, however, it is rarely necessary to voice public opposition to a proposed deal, because the option of just walking away from the transaction is routinely available. But the current structure of the NLRA makes any flat-out refusal to bargain illegal, which in turn makes it entirely appropriate for employers to express their views in the most forceful and authentic terms possible. Why is it improper for employers to point out the fate of so many union workers at the Big Three automakers, or in the steel plants, or anywhere else where union ranks have shrunk with the downturn in business of unionized firms? Why is it inappropriate for small businesses to point to their rivals that have faltered in growth once unionized? The acid test should be whether the statements are true or false. It should not be whether, when true, they are effective or ineffective in influencing worker behavior. The union request for employer detachment is simply a union demand for unilateral employer disarmament in times of conflict. It is a somber truth that once a duty to bargain, found nowhere else, is imposed, employers and unions alike have strong incentives to voice their views with passion and power.

Nor should there be any principled objection to employer speech before a "captive" employee audience, which has long been permitted under the NLRA, except for the 24-hour period immediately preceding an NLRB-conducted secret ballot election. The term "captive" should be put in quotation marks because it does not involve situations where workers are physically restrained. It covers any gatherings of employees on company time while at work. Employer speech in these settings runs the risk of backfiring and, in any event, assembling any required meeting is expensive for an employer, as each of these sessions is on company time. Valuable resources have to be diverted to get that message across. Workers have to be paid to attend these sessions. Indeed, the use of such sessions could easily become more common under a card-check system that leads to compulsory arbitration, for employers know that a card-check drive could be organized at any time. At that point, employers may be well-advised to undertake a permanent campaign to oppose unionization. The stakes of recognition are now higher on both sides. There are no free goods in labor relations. The firm that spends its own resources in opposing a union gives out a strong, unambiguous, costly, and, above all, reliable signal on its views of the consequences of unionization.

The critics of employer speech sidestep these arguments. Their chief objection to employer speech is not that it is illegal but that it is effective. NYU'S Professor Estlund, for example, has protested that one defect of the current electoral campaign, which lasts on average just under six weeks, is that "employers chop away, by legal and illegal means, at the employees' support for the union."[28] Legal and illegal means should never be equated. Holding elections is designed to give employers the chance by *legal* means to do just that, to "chop away" at union support, just as it gives unions a chance to "chop away" at employer support. The standard approaches to deliberative democracy rest on the proposition that the vigorous interchange of ideas allows individuals to reform their choices of means in order to maximize their desired ends. Persuasion is the antithesis of coercion, not its sinister doppelganger. To repeat, so long as illegal routes are not taken, no speech becomes coercive solely because it is effective. The central tenet of the First Amendment is that "the best test of truth is the power of thought to get itself accepted in the competition of the market."[29] When workers change their minds during a campaign, it is not a sign of system pathology. It is a sign of system strength.

In addition, the critics of the current campaign process rarely acknowledge the prominent limitations that section 8(c) of the NLRA places on employer speech. Its final phrase, which permits the speech only "if such expression contains no threat of reprisal or force or promise of benefit," has no analogy anywhere else in First Amendment law. The detailed analysis of what employers or unions may or may not say or do in this area raises a fair number of borderline cases. The rough-and-ready compromise that emerges from

---

28. Estlund statement, supra note 24 (Introduction) at 5.
29. Abrams v. United States, 250 U.S. 616, 630, (1919) (Holmes dissenting).

this provision is that employers may make any statement that accurately reflects the intensity of their opposition to the union. In addition, they may make statements that *predict*, objectively and accurately, the consequences of unionization. But employers cannot provide benefits or promise to grant them as an inducement for employees to remain unrepresented. It is, for example, unlawful under section 8(c) for management to promise certain overtime or vacation benefits just before a union election.[30] Employers may make their case more vivid by showing the business reversals and bankruptcy of formerly successful businesses that have gone the union route. However, one potent tool is taken from them because they are not allowed to make *threats* to either impose costs or remove benefits from workers. To be sure, the firm's CEO can say that "a union contract is likely to make it hard for the firm to compete against" a named rival, but he cannot say pointedly that "if you join a union, I will close the division."

That simple statement conceals underlying complexities, because an employer may in some situations close a plant after a union election, even if it cannot threaten to do so. The leading case on the point remains *Textile Workers Union v. Darlington Manufacturing Co.*[31] which held that section 8(a)(3) governed. In so doing, the U.S. Supreme Court repudiated (as it had to) the common law position that an employer had the absolute right to decide whether to close up shop or remain in business. But at the same time, Justice John Marshall Harlan refused to move to the opposite extreme whereby any decision to close the business necessarily constituted a ULP under section 8(a)(3). Accordingly, he refused to find that any decision to close down a plant, which had the effect of reducing union interests, was an act of coercion governed under section 8(a)(1) of the Act: "A proposition that a single businessman cannot choose to go out of business if he wants to would represent such a startling

---

30. *See, e.g.,* NLRB v. Exchange Parts Co., 375 U.S. 405 (1964).
31. Textile Workers Union v. Darlington Manufacturing Co. 380 U.S. 263 (1965).

innovation that it should not be entertained without the clearest manifestation of legislative intent or unequivocal judicial precedent so construing the Labor Relations Act."[32] Accordingly, *Darlington* adopted a middle position whereby all employer decisions to relocate or subcontract driven by anti-union motivations remain violations of section 8(a)(3) of the NLRA. The language in Section 8(c) is therefore consistent with the dual motivation framework that underlies the Act.

The distinction between a prediction and a threat, implicit in section 8(c), is often difficult to draw in light of verbal slips that arise in the heat of a recognition election. The complexity of this area should caution anyone from reading too much into findings of ULPs in the context of organization drives, discussed in detail later on. The findings reflect only violations of the law; they do not distinguish between the import of statements that say "if you join a union I will close the plant" from "if you join the union, I will beat your brains out in a back alley." Both utterances are illegal under current law, but carry with them different levels of moral turpitude. Nor do these findings indicate whether unlawful statements, especially of the first variety, had any adverse effect on the election in light of all the other campaign activity. But no matter how the findings are interpreted, one point remains: the amount of speech allowed to the employer under current law is far *less* than that allowed to candidates in political elections where all parties are allowed, if not encouraged, to make predictions, threats, and promises with equal abandon, as part of the free, open, and uninhibited debate that is protected under the First Amendment.[33] In other contexts, the only firm limitations on types of speech relate to immediate threats of the use of force. Even fraudulent statements

---

32. *Id.* at 270.

33. *See* New York Times v. Sullivan, 376 U.S. 254, 270–71 (1964). "Authoritative interpretations of the First Amendment guarantees have consistently refused to recognize an exception for any test of truth—whether administered by judges, juries, or administrative officials—and especially one that puts the burden of proving truth on the speaker."

receive some degree of constitutional protection, given the difficulty of disentangling them from true speech in the course of any
political campaign.[34] And the NLRB has flip-flopped on whether
allegations of fraudulent statements should be sufficient to set aside
union elections, precisely because of the difficulty of deciding
whether they actually altered the outcome of the election.[35]

The failure to understand how these rules work often leads union
supporters to postulate improper employer conduct when there is
none. For example, Cornell's Professor Bronfenbrenner insists that
one key determinant of employer success in their anti-union campaigns rests in the threats they make to workers, often covertly, to
take their operations overseas if the union is elected.[36] Bronfenbrenner's reports of covert activities come exclusively from union representatives, who need not be scrupulous about whether the
employers have crossed the wavy line between lawful predictions
and illegal threats.[37] Indeed, in most cases her own descriptions
show that these actions are not illegal under the NLRA. Union
officials understand that they cannot win these cases because the
current law does not treat, as Bronfenbrenner purports to do, as
unlawful "specific unambiguous written threats ranging from

---

34. For an old case in a labor context, see Thomas v. Collins, 323 U.S. 516 (1945). The
state struck down under the First Amendment a state court order that sought to enjoin a
labor union organizer's conviction for failing to obtain a state permit before making a
public speech.

35. See, e.g., Hollywood Ceramics Co., Inc., 140 N.L.R.B. 221, 224 (1962), allowing new
elections on an even-handed standard where misrepresentations "which represent a serious
departure from the truth, at time which prevents the other party or parties from making a
new election; . . ." Shopping Kart Food Market, Inc., 228 N.L.R.B. 1311, 1313 (1977),
restricting new elections to cases that "improperly involve the Board and its processes, or
the use of forged documents which render the voters unable to recognize the propaganda
for what it is." General Knit of California, 239 N.L.R.B. 619 (1978) reverted to the Hollywood Ceramics, only to be reversed yet again in Midland National Life Insurance Co., 263
N.L.R.B. 127 (1982). It is unclear whether either rule systematically favors management or
labor.

36. Kate Bronfenbrenner, Uneasy Terrain: The Impact of Capital Mobility on Workers,
Wages, and Union Organizing. Part II: First Contract Supplement, 10–12 26–28, 55–58
(U.S. Trade Deficit Review Commission 2001).

37. Id. at 7.

newspaper articles, posters, and videos of union plants that had closed, to letters and leaflets which specifically mentioned that the plant would close if the union came in."[38] Given this description, it is not surprising that unions have become "increasingly reluctant to file unfair labor practice charges in response to plant closing threats."[39] Bronfenbrenner uses the word "threat" innumerable times, but the word "prediction" appears only twice in her paper, both in quotations from another source—Human Rights Watch.[40] Her misstatement of the law taints all her empirical conclusions. The material she refers to is all permissible subject matter in a union election. In fact the more systematic neutral studies conclude that in dealing with these campaigns, "the effects of ULP charges were not statistically significant."[41]

Nor is there anything in her broader social claim that these closings have occurred in only 1 percent of the cases in her sample, even if such alleged threats (broadly construed) are made in about half the cases. Her implicit subtext is that these predictions should be regarded as threats because the closing occurs only in a small percentage of cases. But the general context belies the force of her claim. No firm wants to go out of business after unionization. Predictably, unionized firms will try to hold on as long as they can, so long as they have some prospect of a long-term profit. It is no surprise that the low closing rate is found in a study that covered only a two-year period, as there was little time for the plant closings to take place. No long-term effects could be observed. The high number of shuttered plants makes it highly unlikely that the employers have uttered idle words. Indeed, in a prior study Bronfenbrenner notes that for a longer time span, "15 percent of employers actually followed through on the threat and shut down

38. *Id.* at vi.
39. *Id.* at vi.
40. *Id.* at 28.
41. John-Paul Ferguson, The Eyes of the Needles: A Sequential Model of Union Organizing Drives, 1999–2004, 62 Indus. & Lab. Rel. Rev. 1, 14 (2008).

all or part of their operations after the union was voted in."[42] Once again, she misuses the word "threat." But that point aside, her data understate the potential dislocation from unionization. More concretely, we have no idea from this data how many of them contracted operations or refused to expand them.

Union Campaign Advantages

A second side of the coin that needs to be stressed is that labor unions also enjoy significant strategic advantages in election campaigns that have no analogy in a political setting. A concise list of these advantages was offered in the testimony of Charles Cohen, a former member of the NLRB, before the House Subcommittee on Health, Employment, Labor, and Pensions.[43] The first of these is that the union has the advantage of *timing*. It can decide whether to advance or slow down the process, and often does the latter in order to allow its collateral attacks to increase the odds that it will be able to secure a card-check agreement. The second advantage is that it has large control over the *definition* of the bargaining unit for the election. Union support is not uniform in workplaces, and this power of unit designation allows the union to shrink or expand the unit in order to maximize its chances of overall success. Third, on both these critical measures the union has in its *exclusive possession* the signed authorization cards, which supply it with a solid informational base on which to make predictions of the success of various strategies, after which it can force the election within a few weeks. Fourth, once the petition is filed, the union is entitled to receive a *list* of the names and home addresses of all union members. Multiple home visits are permitted to unions but not management. Nothing limits the number of union representatives in any

---

42. Bronfenbrenner, Uneasy Terrain, at 8.

43. *See* Strengthening America's Middle Class Through the Employee Free Choice Act: Hearing on H.R. 800 Before the H. Subcomm. on Health, Employment, Labor, and Pensions, 110th Cong. (2007) (statement of Charles Cohen), available at http://edlabor.house .gov/testimony/020807ChuckCohentestimony.pdf.

particular visit to one. And fifth, unions are *not* bound by the same restrictions that govern employer speech and thus are free to make promises, and often make threats against recalcitrant workers that are difficult to prove or counteract. How this set of advantages squares off against those which employers enjoy is hard to say for sure. But it is clear that the decline in unionization cannot be attributed to any of the rules governing campaigns, which have been stable in form for well over forty years.

SECRET BALLOT VERSUS CARD CHECK

Free Choice or No Choice

The card-check system is even more objectionable because it gives the union the unfettered option to routinely bypass the secret ballot under the NLRA.[44] On this critical issue, the EFCA wraps itself in the mantle of employee free choice. There is, however, no requirement in the EFCA that a union publicly announce that it is undertaking a card-check drive before it begins its efforts to sign up workers, even though one could be easily added. Ironically, it looks as if the EFCA would give a union an option to become the bargaining agent of all workers within a unit as the result of a secret card-check drive whose purpose is to avoid alerting a substantial fraction of fellow workers who are known to be opposed to the union or in support of another union. This pattern might not hold in all cases, as tactical considerations vary. But there is nothing in either the current version of the NLRA or the EFCA that requires public notification before presentation of the signed authorization cards to the Board. To be sure, section 2 of the EFCA does nothing explicitly to limit the ability of employers to speak to employees about their views of the consequences of unionization. And it may

---

44. See George McGovern, My Party Should Respect Union Ballots, Wall St. J., Aug. 8, 2008 at A13.

be possible for employers to engage, at some cost in efficiency and good will, in nonstop campaigns to oppose unions if they perceive that a union campaign is about to begin.

Unions would be in a position, moreover, to make credible charges of employer ULPs if the employer asked employees whether such a secret campaign had begun and, if so, by what union. At present it is probably a ULP for the employer to demand of a worker that he disclose whether a union has started a secret card-check campaign. But it is surely legal for a worker to inform the employer that the campaign is taking place or even for the employer to engage in discussions concerning potential organizing campaigns that workers are free to affirm. This area could easily prove contentious especially if there is no election in the offing. Yet no matter how these countless variations play out, the bottom line is that the EFCA offers a systematic advantage to unions as any secret card-check drive necessarily compromises the employer's ability to target any campaign against the union or unions seeking recognition.

The defenders of the ECFA say little or nothing to justify the possibility of a union preventing dissenting workers from having a voice in the democratic process that the representation elections afford to the union. It is a profound irony that a statute that purports to empower workers to exercise their "free choice" necessarily, and by its own terms, disenfranchises a potentially large fraction of them. The supporters of EFCA have, however, no similar reluctance to denounce the adverse impact that employer speech has on the unionization process. Their view is that employer speech must be misguided because it inhibits the rights of employees to form unions. This, of course, misstates the central objective of the NLRA by ignoring the key language in section 7 of the Act that states in addition to "the right of self-organization," workers "shall also have the right to refrain from any or all such activities" if they choose not to join a union.[45]

---

45. NLRA § 7. (5 U.S.C. § 157).

The truncated card-check policy does more than degrade the deliberative process that leads up to any election. It also exposes workers to multiple forms of intimidation and direct coercion. Today's supporters of the card-check system typically give a polite nod to the virtues of secret elections as a prelude to their all-out attack on all other features of the current electoral system, given the urgency and intensity of the management response.[46] The arguments in support of a card-check program for public employees in Illinois took just that line.[47] Supporters of the card-check policy complain that elections with secret ballots are "lengthy and cumbersome" and that the employer "has control" of the process, meaning that the employer can "routinely" use the campaign period "to scare workers into voting against a union even if the workers want a union."[48] But in their zeal to condemn the employer they never explain why it is necessary to leap to the card-check outcome without figuring out how to expedite or improve union elections within the current framework—which is not easy given the current speed with which they are processed. In so doing, they put on blinders by acting as if all abuses come from the management side. At no point do they discuss, let alone admit, that inherent challenges are associated with an effort to convince employees—who in many cases are already well-compensated— that they should pay money for union representation. Nor do EFCA

46. Strengthening America's Middle Class Through the Employee Free Choice Act: Hearing on H.R. 800 Before the H. Subcomm. on Health, Employment, Labor, and Pensions, 110th Cong. 1–2 (2007) (statement of Gordon Lafer, Associate Professor, University of Oregon) available at http://edworkforce.house.gov/testimony/020807GordonLafertesti mony.pdf.

47. See, Illinois Public Law, 93–444 adding Section 9(a-5), now 5 ILCS 315/9(a-5). Similar provisions for public unions have been added in New York (see N.Y. State Labor Relations Act 20 § 705); New Jersey (see New Jersey Employer-Employee Relations Act 34:13A-5.3); New Hampshire (see Public Employee Labor Relations 22 § 273); Oregon (see Public Employees Rights and Benefits, 243.682); Massachusetts (see Labor Relations: Public Employees, Chap. 105E § 4) ; New Mexico(see New Mexico Statute 10 §7E-14); Ohio (see Ohio Revised Code, Chap 4117) ; and California.

48. Illinois Public Law, 93–444 adding Section 9(a-5), now 5 ILCS 315/9(a-5).

supporters address the allegation that union organizers, or overzea-
lous pro-union employees, are also capable of coercive behavior
during a union election.[49]

Profound doubts over a card check have been voiced by labor's
natural allies. Recently, former Democratic senator and presidential nominee George McGovern condemned EFCA because of its
failure to take into account the obvious: "There are many documented cases where workers have been pressured, harassed,
tricked, and intimidated into signing cards that have led to mandatory payment of dues."[50] And he pointedly asked why it is that
a protection that Americans think desirable outside the United
States should be dispensed with here: "Some of the most
respected Democratic members of Congress—including Reps.
Marcy Kaptur of Ohio, George Miller and Pete Stark of California, and Barney Frank of Massachusetts—have advised workers in
developing countries such as Mexico to insist on the secret ballot
when voting as to whether or not their workplaces should have a
union. We should have no less for employees in our country."[51]
The same position was taken by a former Democratic head of the
NLRB, who recently said that "[s]ecret ballots to resolve union
representation rights are the way to go, and Obama should meet
the Republicans halfway by saying so."[52] And there is little doubt
that all democratic political systems have secret ballots for their
voting decisions. Why then not for union democracy, which is a

---

49. For a more even-handed view of that matter, see Arlen Specter & Eric Nguyen,
Representation without Intimidation: Securing Workers' Right to Choose Under the
National Labor Relations Act, 45 Harv. J. Legis. 312, 319–321 (2008) (union abuses). Id.
321–22.

50. See George McGovern, supra note 44. The letter to which McGovern refers is dated
August 29, 2001 reproduced in the Minority Report to H.R. 800, at 55. George Miller was
the Chairman of the Committee on Labor and Education that produced this report.

51. Id.

52. William B. Gould, IV, How Obama Could Fix Labor Law, Slate, August 29, 2008,
available at http://www.slate.com/id/2198736.

self-conscious progressive effort to introduce similar democratic features into the workplace?[53]

Pressures on the card-check process will be more acute under EFCA than in any public union context because of the size of the stakes. Under EFCA a successful card-check campaign does not lead merely to an election, or even to a collective bargaining negotiation. It leads to "interest" arbitration, whereby union recognition necessarily leads to a guaranteed first contract instead of a union election. Given the stakes, the card-check system may further polarize the union electorate. Pro-union workers will be more committed to the union because they perceive higher rates of return from unionization. But opposing workers may fight harder because they no longer can sign a union authorization card to satisfy an insistent organizer, only to vote against the union in a subsequent election.

Workers who are approached in parks and bars and grocery stores, not even knowing that a campaign is under way, are literally unorganized. They do not know how many other cards have been signed, or whether or how these cards will be validated. But they do know that organizers can have long memories of who is with or against them. These workers could now prefer to capitulate to a union they oppose if the alternative is to be on record against that union when it wins anyhow. If the preference order of these workers is (1) no union, (2) support a union that is likely to be elected,

---

53. *See* for the classic study, Seymour Martin Lipset, Martin Trow & James S. Coleman, *Union Democracy: The Internal Politics of the International Typographical Union* (1956). One recent study notes that the union which Lipset, Trow & Coleman identified as democratic, the International Typographers, still remains the only significant exception. See Samuel Estreicher, Deregulating Union Democracy, 2000 Colum. Bus. Rev. 501, 502–03 (2000). Estreicher's substantive position is to "deregulate" democracy by allowing the union to operate in whatever form it wants, be it as "for-profit firms or oligarchies." Id. 503. Yet the indispensable quid quo pro is "to vote in secret ballot on: (1) authorization of the exclusive bargaining representative; (2) reauthorization at periodic intervals of the bargaining agency; (3) the employer's final contract offer; (4) strike authorization; (5) contract ratification; and (6) the level of fees to be assessed for the bargaining agency (i.e. union dues)." Id. at 503–04. Note that EFCA gives the union that authority without imposing a secret ballot check on any of these critical issues.

or (3) face retaliation if the unwanted union is selected, they could easily choose (2) to avoid (3), even if their first choice is (1). Strategic surrender of this sort would never be made within the confines of a secret ballot.

Unfair Labor Practices in Union Elections

Another key union claim with respect to NLRA secret-ballot elections is that they are undermined by a rash of ULPs. That claim is wrong in two related ways. First, it tends systematically to overstate the number of ULPs that arise during organizing drives. Second, it overlooks the data on election results both for recognition campaigns and for decertification campaigns. Many of the claims for ULPs during union elections are found in the Bronfenbrenner study, which became the centerpiece of the union case that ULPs are the prime culprit in the decline of unionization levels. This study was prepared for the United States Trade Deficit Review Commission, whose major purpose was to deliver a strong protectionist message. In Bronfenbrenner's view, globalization is the major threat that any successful national labor policy should resist.[54] Her major conclusion is that employer threats to take business overseas are a chief source of labor insecurity, which triggers a "race to the bottom" in "working conditions and living standards" that only strong union action can counteract.[55] At no point does the study show the slightest recognition that competition is generally a source of higher productivity and lower prices, which have precisely the opposite effect. Nor does she recognize the risk of collapse which is an inherent risk of this aggressive strategy. Writing in 2000, she singled out the automobile industry as one of the few sectors that had held its ground on wage issues.[56] Her study reveals no

---

54. Kate Bronfenbrenner, supra note 36 at 55.
55. *Id.* at viii.
56. *Id.* at 11.

inkling of the chaos among the Big Three manufacturers that was to follow, with the loss of 500,000 jobs. Nor could she have anticipated the jockeying for a massive bailout program, which at this writing is calling for an infusion of billions of dollars into General Motors, and Chrysler with the active cooperation of management and United Auto Workers officials, including its president, Ronald Gettelfinger.[57] Nor does she mention that foreign automobile manufacturers in the United States have remained profitable with worker wages around $26 per hour[58].

Armed with her flawed world view, Bronfenbrenner then examines a random sample of 600 certification elections conducted by the NLRB, creating a data set that rests exclusively on the evaluations of the "lead organizers" of these campaigns,[59] without any cross check to either official or employer records to see whether the reported violations were correctly characterized. Her collection method of the survey data is in itself sufficient reason to discredit her results in their entirety.

But even putting that obvious methodological objection to the side, a closer look at her data reveals how the bias in data collection works its way through the argument. One of her claims is that "one in four employers in our sample discharged workers for union activity."[60] This glass could be regarded as at least three-quarters empty, especially since "[u]nions won 44 percent of all the elections in the sample and 38 percent of elections with threats."[61] The differential rate is sufficiently small that it could hardly explain more than a tiny fraction of major decline in union representation over the past fifty years. If each election accounted for about one hundred workers, then the 6 percent differential over 600 cases translates into thirty-six additional union victories, or 3,600 workers

57. Testimony of Mark Zandi, before U.S. Senate Banking Committee, "The State of the Domestic Auto Industry: Part II" December 4, 2008.

58. David Leonhardt, $73 an Hour: Adding It Up, N.Y. Times, Dec. 9, 2008 at A1.

59. Kate Bronfenbrenner, supra note 36, at 12.

60. Id. at 43.

61. Id. at 51.

who should have been unionized in this sample. But even that differential is overstated because it does not give any offset for the NLRB-ordered reinstatements to workers who were determined to be subject to those practices—a figure that cannot be accurately determined from Bronfenbrenner's reports.[62]

Nor are there major changes in the overall landscape if these figures are projected over the entire set of union elections. Assuming that this figure is accurate—which it is not—it translates into an increase over the eight-year period of 2000 to 2008 into about 75,000 additional union members, which is 6 percent of the roughly 1,250,000 individuals who participated in these elections.[63] That figure has to be reduced further to take into account those cases in which the union is unable to bargain to a first contract, and those in which the union certification led to attrition in the total size of the workforce. The numbers are too small, with any reasonable adjustments, to account for the decline in union membership.

The more important errors in Bronfenbrenner's study relate to the computation of the data set in the first place, for it is always difficult to figure out which ULPs filed in the midst of a certification election were filed with respect to practices undertaken during that election. As noted below, NLRB data reveal that more than 90 percent of NLRB elections are held within sixty days after the union representation petition is filed. The NLRA section 10(b), however, allows the filing of unfair labor practices up to six months following the conduct that is alleged to be unlawful.[64]

On this score, the overtly pro-management analysis provided by J. Justin Wilson of the Center for Union Facts differs from Bronfenbrenner's in that it does not rely on survey data collected from

---

62. The numbers are impossible to determine from Bronfenbrenner's data because she states that "unions won at least a complaint or a settlement for 70 percent of all charges filed, or 23 percent of all election campaigns during 1998–1999." The numbers do not quite add up because relief in 23 percent of the election campaigns translates to relief in 98 percent of the election campaigns in which, by her assumptions, ULPs were filed.

63. *See* Table 2, infra at 53.

64. Section 10(b), 29 U.S.C. §160(b),

union organizers—or, for that matter, interested employers. Instead, its sole data source is the information systematically gathered from official NLRB records—its Case Activity Tracking System (CATS) database—on both the conduct of union organization campaigns and the distribution of ULPs.[65] The interpretation of the data requires a detailed examination of individual cases to match any ULP to a particular campaign, for the CATS reports do not divide their reinstatement cases between those tied to union organization drives and those connected with other sorts of activity. Wilson performed detailed matches on name similarity to sort the ULPs by category.[66] Even that adjustment tends to bias upward the number of ULPs committed during the organizational drives, because it cannot distinguish in firms that have multiple bargaining units the particular cases that were attributable to its organizational and its other activities. Nonetheless, Wilson concluded that over the three-year period from 2003 to 2005—using data that are more recent and more comprehensive than Bronfenbrenner's—11,342 organizing petitions were filed. During that period, workers were offered reinstatement through remedial action in 3,675 cases. Some remedial action was taken in 1,538 of the 3,546 CA cases (i.e., ULP cases filed against employers) filed in conjunction with the 11,342 CA petitions. At the same time, 608 cases were dismissed, and 1,400 cases were withdrawn. Of the 1,538 CA cases in which remedial actions were taken, only 303 arose in the course of an organization campaign. Accordingly, there were 303 improper firings for the 11,342 organizing campaigns, implying that the likelihood of an improper firing by an employer during the course of a union campaign is only 2.7 percent.[67]   The large number of withdrawn cases—40 percent of the total—may have been filed for strategic

---

65. *See* J. Justin Wilson, Union Math, Union Myths: An Analysis of Government Data on Employees Fired During Union Organizing Campaigns, Center for Union Facts, June 2007, available at www.unionfacts.com/downloads/Union_Math_Union_Myths.pdf.

66. *Id.* at 3–4

67. *Id.* at 9, and Table 4.

reasons only. It is a far cry from Bronfenbrenner's 25 percent figure. To be sure, Wilson's numbers could be low if some workers chose not to file valid grievances with the NLRB. But by the same token, these data are consistent with another message: it is bad strategy for reputational reasons to fire workers during a campaign, and management lawyers constantly warn employers of the business risks they take, apart from any legal sanctions that might be imposed.

The Bronfenbrenner study is not the only one that overestimates the level of illegal employer behavior in organizational campaigns. An earlier study by Paul Weiler, a Harvard law professor and AFL-CIO board member in both the United States and Canada, reported that employers had fired 5 percent of the pro-union employees during an organization campaign, which would amount to thousands of workers per year.[68] That figure was forcefully challenged in a paper by Robert LaLonde and my late University of Chicago Law School colleague Professor Bernard D. Meltzer, who reduced that figure to one in sixty-three pro-union workers, or about 1.59 percent, on the assumption that only 50 percent of all cases in which reinstatement was sought were for organizational activities.[69] Wilson, however, disputes their claim that half of the NLRB reinstatement orders come from organizing campaigns, which he found (with some adjustments for card checks) was roughly 10 percent for the 2003 to 2005 data. He recalculates the number of dismissals on the assumption that only 10 percent of the reinstatements were for organizational assumptions, at which point the number drops to about one in 340 pro-union workers, or 0.295 percent, a number so small that it hardly suggests a major problem that operates as a systematic deterrence to union organization.

---

68. *See* Paul Weiler, Promises to Keep: Securing Workers' Rights to Self Organization under the NLRA, 96 Harv. L. Rev. 1769, 1781 (1983).

69. Robert J. LaLonde & Bernard D. Meltzer, Hard Times for Unions: Another Look at the Significance of Employer Illegalities, 58 U.Chi. L. Rev. 953 (1991).

We can analyze the role of ULPs in other ways. Bronfenbrenner notes that the longer election campaigns take, the less likely the union is to prevail. She reports the union's rate of success is 50 percent for elections held within sixty days of the filing of the petition, but only 31 percent for elections held from sixty-one to 180 days after the filing of the petition.[70] Ironically, when put into context, this evidence cuts *in favor* of the probity of the current system of union elections. NLRB General Counsel Ronald Meisburg has two instructive findings in his 2007 report of NLRB activity: "Initial elections in union representation elections were conducted in a median of thirty-nine days from the filing of the petition."[71] "93.9 percent of all initial representation elections were conducted within fifty-six days of the filing of the petition in FY 2007, compared to 94.1 percent in FY 2006, and above our target of 90 percent."[72] It is clear that the second figure of 31 percent success covers something under 6 percent of the elections, so that all the institutional weight attaches to the first figure. Even so, there is a lingering misconception about the delays in setting these elections. William B. Gould IV, head of the NLRB during President Clinton's administration, believes that these elections should be staged "within one or two weeks of the filing of a union's petition seeking recognition,"[73] which seems short given the number of elections and the inevitable difficulties in their administration. But he makes this recommendation on the incorrect assumption that "the resolution of union drives currently takes months and sometimes years."[74] The promptness of the elections makes it difficult to subject them to any real attack.

---

70. Kate Bronfenbrenner, supra note 6, at 78–79.

71. Memorandum GC 08–01, December 5, 2007, Summary of Operations (Fiscal Year 2007), at 1. http://www.nlrb.gov/shared_files/GC Memo/2008/GC 08–01 Summary of Operations FY 07.pdf

72. *Id.* at 6.

73. William B. Gould, supra note 52.

74. *Id.*

ELECTION RESULTS

The conclusion that ULPs have little impact on the rate of unionization is confirmed by looking at the tabulations that the NLRB supplies with respect to organizing campaigns between April 2000 and March 2008. The data indicate that of 17,870 collective bargaining elections, unions won 10,148, or about 56.8 percent. These elections involved a total of about 1,253,000 workers for an average of about seventy workers per unit. The union victories yielded a net of 585,150 workers, for about fifty-eight workers per unit. The union defeats covered 668,235 workers in 7,722 units for an average of about eighty-seven workers per unit. The most striking feature about the data is the reduction in union elections between April 2000 and March 2008, coupled with their increased success rate.

These data reflect two major trends. The first is that the number of elections has declined over the past eight years. It appears to be the unions' judgment that their alternative tactics for securing representation are more effective, so that they resort to elections only in settings where their prospects are more favorable. Second, the small size of the relevant units suggests that most of the targeted employers are themselves small businesses, even if some of them exceed the customary definition of a small business as one with fewer than 100 employees. The figures vary from year to year, but the basic pattern is summarized in the following graphs which indicate by unit size the number of workers in which the union and the employer prevailed in elections, where labor sought representation, and elections held to see whether a union would be decertified.

The volume of elections is sufficiently high to suggest that unions did not perceive any insuperable obstacles in conducting their organizing campaigns. The divided outcomes suggest that employers were also able to make their case in some instances but by no means in all. There is no evidence of which I am aware that indicates that employer resistance has aborted a substantial number of organizational campaigns that might have succeeded in the absence

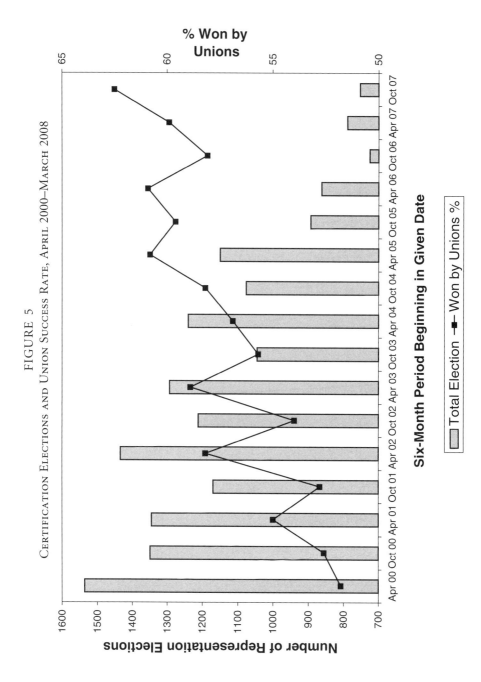

FIGURE 5

CERTIFICATION ELECTIONS AND UNION SUCCESS RATE, APRIL 2000–MARCH 2008

TABLE 3
CERTIFICATION ELECTIONS 2003–2006 BY SIZE OF UNIT (RC & RM)

Size of Unit (number of employees)	2003 Representation Chosen	2003 NO Representation Chosen	2004 Representation Chosen	2004 NO Representation Chosen	2005 Representation Chosen	2005 NO Representation Chosen	2006 Representation Chosen	2006 NO Representation Chosen
Under 10	365	165	311	153	294	159	322	117
10 to 19	304	214	269	173	347	148	205	120
20 to 29	175	140	136	141	192	137	129	94
30 to 39	99	90	108	91	118	61	85	71
40 to 49	80	58	67	56	61	63	53	55
50 to 59	63	64	54	63	52	41	43	38
60 to 69	43	44	51	38	30	40	35	25
70 to 79	39	36	40	29	34	21	18	23
80 to 89	37	36	38	17	27	37	19	25
90 to 99	28	22	28	23	24	18	18	18
Under 100	1,233	869	1,102	784	1,179	725	927	586
Over 100	185	225	187	210	161	168	139	122
Total	1,418	1,094	1,289	994	1,340	893	1,066	708

RC: A petition filed by a labor organization or an employee alleging that a question concerning representation has arisen and seeking an election for determination of a collective-bargaining representative.

RM: A petition filed by an employer alleging that a question concerning representation has arisen and seeking an election for the determination of a collective-bargaining representative.

TABLE 4
Union Certification Elections

Period	Elections Participated in			Eligible Employees to Vote in		
	Total	Resulting in Certification	No Representation Chosen	Total	Units that Selected Representation	Units that Chose No Representation
Oct 07–Mar 08	752	470	282	49,411	29,018	20,393
Apr 07–Sept 07	788	472	316	48,240	26,717	21,523
Oct 06–Mar 07	725	421	304	51,905	30,018	21,887
Apr 06–Sept 06	862	525	337	61,040	30,849	30,191
Oct 05–Mar 06	893	532	361	62,103	36,253	25,850
Apr 05–Sept 05	1,150	699	451	72,495	34,708	37,787
Oct 04–Mar 05	1,076	626	450	77,104	34,062	43,042
Apr 04–Sept 04	1,240	705	535	83,094	40,440	42,654
Oct 03–Mar 04	1,045	582	463	79,341	38,232	41,109
Apr 03–Sept 03	1,293	762	531	78,945	41,372	37,573
Oct 02–Mar 03	1,212	655	557	88,478	34,301	54,177
Apr 02–Sept 02	1,434	835	599	89,181	45,020	44,161
Oct 01–Mar 02	1,170	618	552	85,664	34,094	51,570
Apr 01–Sept 01	1,345	740	605	105,351	38,008	67,343
Oct 00–Mar 01	1,349	710	639	101,788	41,269	60,519
Apr 00–Sept 00	1,536	796	740	119,245	50,789	68,456

of any ULPs. The more likely explanation for the recent decline in union representation is the rise of neutrality agreements and card-check campaigns.

Decertification elections reinforce the story, as illustrated in Table 5. Here no card check is allowed to decertify a union. The primary route is through elections called for by unit employees; in some instances an employer can withdraw recognition of a majority union if it can show, not just a good faith doubt as to the position of the union, but "the union's actual loss of majority status."[75] As might be expected, these elections are far less frequent than certification elections. In addition, the units in question are not selected at random, but for their history of poor or corrupt union relations. Again, the results show no sign of process breakdown. The results are closely contested both in terms of units and in terms of votes. The results thus confirm the general view that the electoral process works more or less as it should.

In any event, the influence of these elections on the overall level of unionization in the workforce is small, for even if the unions had won all of the contested elections, the additional 668,235 workers are less than the overall decline in union membership during the same period. The results hardly change if it were deemed proper for the union to overcome all the successful decertification elections. If all these workers were, over an eight-year period, put back into the mix, the total of union workers would have increased only to 8,890,000, equal to the sum of the number of union members in private industry in 2007 (8,114,000) plus the 668,235 workers in units where the union lost a recognition election and the 105,637 employees who were in decertified units. This still leads to only an 8.2 percent unionization rate in the private sector workforce. These figures provide the maximum because they assume that all the union defeats were improper and, further, that all these additional

---

75. *See* Levitz Furniture Company of the Pacific, Inc.333 NLRB No. 105 (2001).

FIGURE 6

CERTIFICATION ELECTIONS—REPRESENTATION CHOSEN, 2003–2006

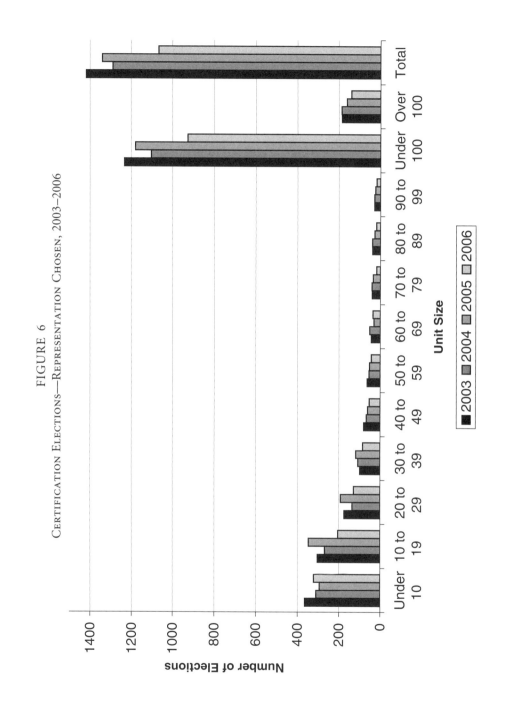

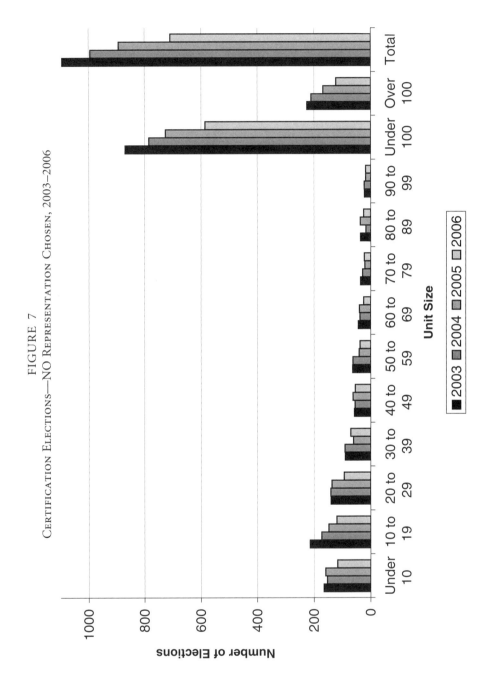

FIGURE 7

CERTIFICATION ELECTIONS—NO REPRESENTATION CHOSEN, 2003–2006

TABLE 5
DECERTIFICATION ELECTIONS

Period	Elections Participated in			Valid Votes Cast		
	Total	Resulting in Certification	Resulting in Decertification	Total	Cast for the Union	Cast Against the Union
Oct 07–Mar 08	149	63	86	9,505	5,456	4,049
Apr 07–Sept 07	190	65	125	13,257	6,646	6,611
Oct 06–Mar 07	165	58	107	8,245	4,726	3,519
Apr 06–Sept 06	181	58	123	10,364	5,230	5,134
Oct 05–Mar 06	176	58	118	13,365	7,810	5,555
Apr 05–Sept 05	158	55	103	10,775	6,264	4,511
Oct 04–Mar 05	220	74	146	10,923	5,324	5,599
Apr 04–Sept 04	208	68	140	9,562	4,717	4,845
Oct 03–Mar 04	212	78	134	15,395	7,225	8,170
Apr 03–Sept 03	194	72	122	10,150	5,059	5,091
Oct 02–Mar 03	226	78	148	13,845	6,297	7,548
Apr 02–Sept 02	228	63	165	9,870	4,487	5,383
Oct 01–Mar 02	188	67	121	7,365	3,649	3,716
Apr 01–Sept 01	195	71	124	12,082	6,706	5,376
Oct 00–Mar 01	167	50	117	9,702	4,950	4,752
Apr 00–Sept 00	207	69	138	11,276	5,731	5,545

workers would have retained their jobs, in the face of the strong competitive pressures that have led to national declines.

In recent years the decline in union membership has outstripped the gains from new elections. The second column of Table 6 shows the gain or loss in the existing ranks. The third column shows the number of new union members. The reduction in the existing ranks over this period equals 2,559,000 members, which again dwarfs the 668,000 individuals who voted not to join a union during that period. Stated otherwise, union membership losses after attrition would have equaled about 1,786,000 members even if the unions had won every single recognition and decertification election. Given the expansion of the overall workforce, the percentage declines in union membership are best understood as a lack of demand for union representation and not a defect in the election process.

The evidence is overwhelming that the decline of the labor movement is not attributable to any defect, real or imagined, in the present election process. Among the many potential explanations, two features emerge. The first is the erosion in membership of the once-dominant unions such as the United Auto Workers, the Steel-workers, and the Rubber Workers. As Figure 8 shows, these three unions today have about 1.5 million fewer members than they did during the mid-1970s—and even that number will decline no matter what happens to the proposed federal bailout of the former Big Three. The uptick in United Steelworkers membership that we see in recent years is primarily due to mergers of other unions with USW, including the Rubber Workers and PACE Union, artificially raising USW membership by over 340,000 members.[76]

The second factor is the inability of union firms to grow relative to their nonunion competitors in such key sectors as retailing, which in principle should present attractive targets for unioniza-tion. This point is of special importance because it suggests that the

---

76. URW had 80,000 members in 1995, before its merger with USW; PACE's member-ship stood at about 260,000 members in 2005.

TABLE 6

UNION MEMBERSHIP 2000–2007: SOME PRIVATE SECTOR STATISTICS

Year	Number of Union Members (000's)	Loss of Current Membership from Prior Year (000's)	New Members through Elections (000's)*	Net Change in Membership from Prior Year (000's)	Size of Workforce (000's)	% of Workforce Unionized
2000	9,148	−492	221	−271	101,810	9.0%
2001	9,113	−226	191	−35	101,605	9.0%
2002	8,800	−491	178	−313	102,153	8.6%
2003	8,452	−506	158	−348	102,648	8.2%
2004	8,205	−407	160	−247	103,584	7.9%
2005	8,255	−85	135	50	105,508	7.8%
2006	7,981	−387	113	−274	107,846	7.4%
2007	8,114	35	98	133	108,714	7.5%

*Year is considered from April to March of following year.

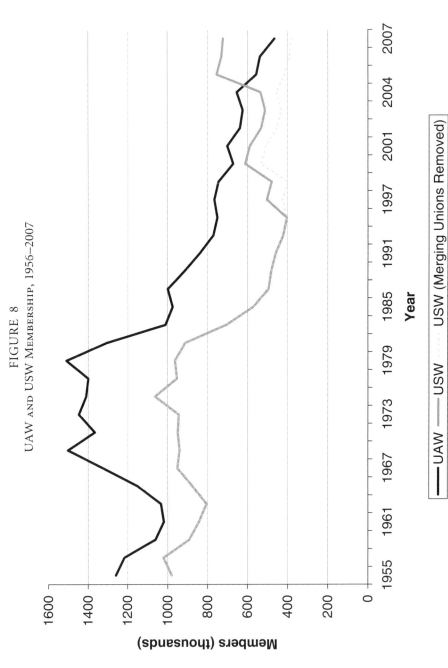

FIGURE 8
UAW and USW Membership, 1956–2007

Members (thousands)

Year

—— UAW —— USW ········ USW (Merging Unions Removed)

Note that in removing merged unions, it is assumed that the membership of those unions is stable over time. Also note that we are only removing the PACE and URW membership.

consequences of unionization for small firms should not be evaluated solely in terms of the number of workers who are unionized each year. The key question is the extent to which unionization of small firms inhibits the potential for growth so that these firms do not realize their full economic potential. It is instructive to note that the explosive growth in the retail sector is concentrated in such nonunionized retail firms as Publix and Target. Publix has seen its workforce expand from 82,000 to 144,000 between 1993 and 2007. Target grew from 174,000 to 366,000 workers during that same period. I am not aware of any unionized firm that can show that kind of sustained growth over a parallel stretch of time.

The reason is not hard to find. The standard union mantra is that gains of this sort are possible within the union framework if only the management team would work in "partnership" with its union. But this mellow approach misconceives the nature of partnerships, which in business matters can only arise from voluntary arrangements and only last so long as the atmosphere of trust survives between the parties. Partners do not rely on litigation and arbitration during the course of their business. They only use it when the business has come apart. No employer-union relationship can meet that standard of voluntary cooperation under a statutory scheme that imposes duties to bargain. The entire system of collective bargaining results in the following paradox, whereby traditional conceptions of good faith—the touchstone in partnership law—can only exist within a voluntary framework that is inconsistent with the very different brand of "good faith" negotiations contemplated under the labor statutes. No system of divided control under the present mandatory regime can generate the level of trust needed for the kind of voluntary cooperation that is the hallmark of genuine business partnerships. Rather, the length and complexity of collective bargaining agreements and the long periods for their negotiations offer powerful proof why the growth of unionized firms will lag behind that of their well-run nonunionized rivals. In the present age of austerity, to sacrifice potential jobs for the flawed

FIGURE 9
URW Membership, 1956–1995

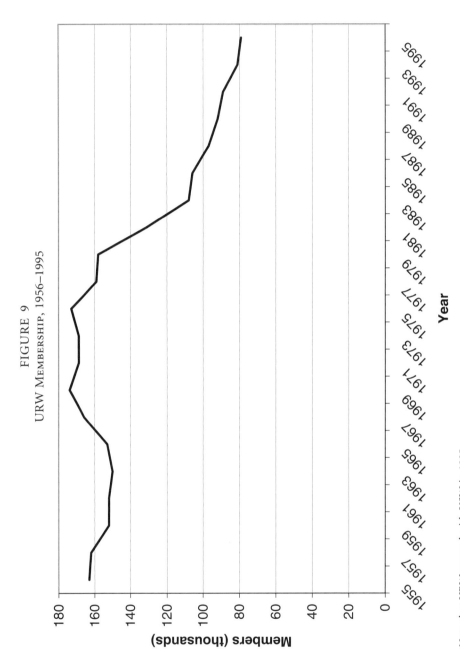

Members (thousands)

Year

Note that URW merged with USW in 1995.

ideal of greater union penetration into employment markets is to kill jobs on Main Street in support of an ideal that is preserved only because of the misguided ingenuity of strong union supporters. EFCA will only magnify the disadvantages of the current system of labor relations.

The Infirmities of Card-Check Campaigns

Card Checks Under the Current Law

The use of the card check will surely change these calculations, by shutting off input from both dissenting workers and the employer, especially if the campaign can begin in secret. Some reports suggest that organizing campaigns enjoy a 78 percent success rate when the neutrality agreement institutes card checks and imposes limits on employer speech.[77] If these numbers are to be taken at face value, the choice of rules makes a difference in outcomes. Start with the position of unit members. As previously noted, so long as an election is required, the effort of unions to turn to their supporters for card checks has only limited effects. The unions understand this as well. The collection of card signatures can take place at any time and any place. It is wholly unsupervised by the Board or anyone else. Under the current law, once a union obtains signatures from 30 percent of workers, the formal NLRB recognition process can begin.[78] As the gains to a union from satisfying the card check are limited, the willingness of a union to use tactics that involve intimidation or misrepresentation is lower as well. Those who disagree with the union need not mark themselves for criticism, for they can sign the card and then vote against the union in the election by secret ballot. That election takes place after a campaign. All workers

---

77. Brudney II, supra note 5, at 13.

78. Based on 30 percent figure for having a representation election. NLRA § 9(c)(1). (5 U.S.C. § 159(c)(1)).

are in a position to make their views known to their fellow workers at any time during the election campaign, including those coworkers who have previously signed the cards. The fact that such speech could sway workers against a union is the reason why it should be allowed. The essence of a free and robust debate is the risk that the arguments of your opponents will prove more persuasive to the electorate than your own.

Nor, finally, is there any theoretical reason to doubt the empirical results that show at most mixed union success in NLRB elections. We should expect employer speech—and potential opposition expressed by some employees themselves—to be persuasive at least some of the time. After all, employers can often make their case in ways that make their opposition resonate with the legitimate concerns of their employees. As with all complex choices, the decision to join a union has the potential for both advantages and disadvantages. In brief, prospective union membership does not come cheap. Unions impose dues and service obligations; they impose hidden barriers that hamper the advancement of able members of the rank and file into management; rules create implicit conflicts between workers in different groups, whether measured by age, length of service, or occupation; union work rules render firms less nimble to meet competition and to adopt new technologies; union firms are subject to disruptions by strikes, lockouts, and slowdowns in which aggressive union tactics can in fact kill the employer goose that lays the golden egg. Rational and informed workers could therefore conclude that the full costs of union membership exceed its benefits to *them*, without regard to any larger social consequences. These workers have no incentive to support a union that does not advance their interests solely because that union also disadvantages the employer. The mixed results in union elections are an accurate reflection of those competing forces.

The entire calculus of costs and rewards changes under the proposed card-check system of EFCA. Now the union gains to card collection are far greater: the union becomes the designated bargaining agent when it obtains cards from a majority of the members of the unit. An astute union will no longer find it necessary to announce an organization campaign with great fanfare. Rather, in most if not all cases unions will proceed surreptitiously to circumvent opposing employees and round up as many cards as possible in a silent phase of its campaign. At this point the risks of employee intimidation and misrepresentation from unsupervised union conduct are far greater. These tactics yield the union a greater gain once the backstop of the supervised election is eliminated. It is all too easy for union organizers to trap with impunity workers in dark hallways or on isolated streets after dark. There are countless contexts in which the threat of coercion can be implicit, powerful, and unreported. The fear of revenge from a successful union is not something that many workers can view with indifference. The change in the payoff from a victorious card check will lead to a change for the worse in how unions conduct their organizing campaigns. The large gains from getting signed cards, and the easy means to obtain them, could well raise union abuse to levels above those in the current system.

The situation is aggravated still further once these cards are turned over to the union. Existing law treats union authorization cards as irrevocable. Nor does it supply any effective mechanism that allows employees to revoke or withdraw their authorization cards, once signed. The NLRB has written: "A showing of interest is not subject to attack on the ground that the cards on which it is based have been revoked or withdrawn. Such an attack . . . has no bearing on the validity of the original showing but merely raises the question as to whether particular employees have changed their minds about union representation. That question can best be resolved on the basis of an election by secret ballot."[79] The curative

---

79. NLRB, Outline of Law and Procedure in Representation Cases § 5–400, pp. 44–45 (July 2005), quoting General Dynamics Corp., 175 NLRB 1035 (1969).

power of the secret ballot is not available under the EFCA. Also under existing law, authorization cards may be regarded as current for a year or more after being signed.[80] And authorization card signatures, under existing law, "are presumed to be genuine unless there is some indication to the contrary."[81] Moreover, employers under existing law in representation proceedings *cannot even litigate* questions about the production of fabricated or fraudulent authorization cards.[82] At most they may submit to the NLRB regional director any evidence of fraudulent or fabricated authorization cards. Even that information is difficult to assemble because the NLRB does not release to the employer its information about which employees reportedly signed the authorization cards submitted to the NLRB.[83] The administrative remedy dominates.[84]

Use of these truncated procedures has more dire consequences under EFCA, for now they are not backstopped by a secret ballot election. To be sure, EFCA charges the NLRB with developing procedures for establishing "the validity of signed authorizations designating bargaining representatives" (EFCA § 2). It is worth noting

---

80. Outline of Law and Procedure in Representation Cases § 5–500, p. 45 (July 2005), citing Carey Mfg. Co., 69 NLRB 224 n. 4 (1946); Northern Trust Co., 69 NLRB 652 n. 4 (1946).

81. NLRB, Outline of Law and Procedure in Representation Cases § 5–400, p. 44 (July 2005).

82. *See, e.g.,* NLRB, Outline of Law and Procedure in Representation Cases § 5–900, p. 48 (July 2005), quoting S. H. Kress & Co., 137 NLRB 1244, 1248–1249 (1962): "An integral and essential element of the Board's showing-of-interest rule is the non-litigability of a petitioner's evidence as to such interest. The Board reserves to itself the function of investigating such claims, and in its investigation it endeavors to keep the identity of the employees involved secret from the employer and other participating labor organizations. . . . The Board's requirement that petitions be supported by a 30-percent showing of interest gives rise to no special obligation or right on the part of employers."

83. *Id.*

84. By way of contrast, the legal position is quite different under the age discrimination laws, which provides that release agreements for age discrimination claims are only enforceable under federal law if the agreement explicitly states that the employee is entitled to revoke it for a period of at least seven days after it is signed. That protection follows an earlier period during which employees are guaranteed at least 21 days (45 days in situations involve a "group" program) to review the agreement in light of other disclosures now mandated under federal law. The level of protection is all too dependent on context. *See,*

that all efforts by the Republican minority in Congress to bulk up EFCA procedures with additional protections for the card check were opposed by all Democrats on the committee.[85]

One such proposal would require union officials to return a card within five days after a request by an employee. That approach would permit workers to update their preferences before the card may be submitted. Otherwise the process results in a systematic tilt toward the union. If a worker at any time signs the card, then he is bound for the duration of the period. There could be a successful card authorization program, even though the requisite numbers of workers do not support the program at the time it is submitted. Take a simple example: if 60 percent of workers sign cards over the course of a campaign, and 20 percent wish them back at the end, the union prevails with 40 percent support when it chooses, on its own initiative, to submit the cards to the NLRB.

A second proposal would have limited the card check to workers who had been employed for at least 180 days, in order to eliminate salted workers from voting, and to establish some permanent connection with the work force. That proposal would have the advantage of blocking the use of card checks for newly formed firms that were not in existence for 180 days, in order to prevent a simple majority of the incumbent workers from binding new workers who had no opportunity to participate in the deliberations at all.

A third proposal would have limited card-check authorizations to persons who are legally in the United States, and thus prevent illegal aliens from influencing or perhaps controlling the outcome of the card check. There are of course serious questions of how illegal aliens should be treated under labor law, on which I venture no opinion here. But it does seem odd that so long as these workers

---

e.g., 29 U.S.C. § 626(f) (Older Workers Benefit Protection Act amendments to federal Age Discrimination in Employment Act).

85. *See* Minority Views, Report on the Employee Free Choice Act of 2007 (H.R. 800) Report 110–23, at 58–59.

are at risk for deportation they should be given a say—perhaps the decisive say—in whether a firm should be unionized.

A fourth proposal provided that reinstatement could not be ordered for union workers who engaged in violence or other dangerous behavior. A complementary proposal called for the decertification of any union that encouraged or used violence, in line with the NLRA's policy to promote industrial peace. The refusal to adopt this provision shows the implicit double standard in a statute that beefs up sanctions against employers for conduct found to be a ULP, including that which falls far short of the serious abuses here.

Even if all these proposals were adopted they would not, in my view, make the card-check system preferable to the secret ballot election, with its long history of institutional safeguards. The established law on secret ballot elections goes to great pains to prevent either side from disrupting the process. The basic NLRB standard strives to achieve "laboratory" conditions to rule out the possibility of abuse.[86] Standard rules require that employers post three days before elections posters that inform workers of their rights. Electioneering is prohibited near the election site. The elections are conducted by neutral NLRB officials, under the scrutiny of observers from both employer and employees. The eligibility of voters is established by list prior to the election. The NLRB agents maintain physical custody over the ballot box at all times, and remove it from the premises when the election is completed.

Experience in states where there are public employee card-check recognition regimes provides little hope that the regulations under EFCA would sensibly address these numerous deficiencies. Under the Illinois public sector collective bargaining statute, for example, union authorization cards are *not* revocable for a six-month period, even at the request of the worker.[87] Hence any reduction in prounion sentiment will have a smaller effect in the card-check context

---

86. *See* General Shoe Corp., 77 NLRB 124, 126–27 (1948).
87. Illinois Administrative Code 80 § 1210.80.

than in an electoral one. The campaign in its public phase also works with a one-way ratchet so that formerly anti-union workers can change their mind at any time within the six-month window, while formerly pro-union workers cannot. It is quite easy to see today why a union that wins a card-check campaign could, as often happens, lose the subsequent election. It is hard to imagine any process that is less democratic in either intention or execution than the card-check rule under EFCA. The only clear winner of this skewed and expedited process is the union leadership, which gains dues and power through the successful certification campaign.

Selective Use of Card Checks

There is a second telltale sign of the dubious legitimacy of the card-check system. Under section 2 of EFCA, its use is reserved to only one situation: the selection of a union for a workforce that is not organized. Supporters of EFCA would regard it as ludicrous to allow employers to collect signed cards from workers that indicate their preference not to have a union. And defenders of EFCA would bristle at any suggestion that a later employer card could displace a signature on a prior union card. But they do not explain why the risks of coercion by employers are greater in the one case than in the other.

In addition, the drafters of EFCA did not propose a system of card-check decertification that would take effect if 30 percent of the workers within an appropriate bargaining unit signed cards asking for the decertification of an incumbent union. That result can, however, be grafted on to the card-check system. The NLRB took just this position in its 2007 decision in *Dana Corp.* which involved two cases of businesses whose workers expressed strong sentiments against the union card check.[88] At issue in that case were two successful union card-check campaigns on which the respective unions

---

88. 351 NLRB No. 28 (2007).

sought immediate orders to negotiate. In both cases, dissident workers filed petitions to hold an immediate decertification election. In one instance, the petition was signed by a majority of workers in the unit. In the other case, 35 percent signed, which is greater than the 30 percent requirement of cards to trigger an election. The usual rule where a union is certified through an election is to create a recognition bar that lasts for three years, during which period the union can negotiate a contract, without fear of facing a dissident election for decertification.[89] The need for this rule follows from the fluctuating membership of any bargaining unit over the protracted period of bargaining between employer and union. By analogy to political elections, the results stand even though shifts in electoral composition or sentiment follow Election Day. No one questions the need for this recognition bar in electoral contexts.

Card-check certification, however, does not have the same probative weight as a union election, so the much mooted question is whether the same recognition bar should attach in the new context. Once again, a sharply divided Board held that the infirmities of the card check, with its attendant risks of mistake, fraud, confusion, and coercion, did not justify the automatic progression from majority signatures to Board recognition. Instead, it created by administrative rule (which any new Board could easily undo) a new procedure that allows for an election so long as 30 percent of the workers within the unit call for it, which is the same percentage needed to trigger an election today. The fact that the anti-union forces could gather that number of votes within a short time offers some evidence of the weak probative value of card checks. Once the union survives the recognition election, the automatic three-year recognition bar applies as in other cases.

It is doubtful whether this administrative correction survives under EFCA, which simply provides that the Board "shall" order

---

89. *See, e.g.,* Keller Plastics Eastern, Inc. 157 NLRB 583 (1966).

the parties to bargain. But it makes no provision for employees to present their rival cards within 45 days of the original filing to trigger an election. Instead, it appears that EFCA would leave untouched the current process under which unit employees must wait to request a decertification election under various complex rules that kick in either on the expiration of a short-term union contract or after three years under a union contract that runs three or more years. Given the pro-union bias of EFCA, it is not likely that many courts would think that the NRLB could preserve its rule in *Dana Corp.*, even if it were inclined to do so.

Another conspicuous problem with EFCA is the absence of any explicit provision stating that a failed card-check campaign can't be immediately followed by a new campaign, either by the original or a second union. The current version of the NLRA only provides that a new election cannot be ordered "in any bargaining unit within which in the preceding twelve-month period, a valid election shall have been held."[90] There is no conforming amendment that would raise this bar against new check-card drives after either a previous election within that twelve-month period or a failed card-check drive within that time (assuming that it goes far enough to become public knowledge). Employers and dissenting workers can be subject to multiple attacks along this front.

The most telling provision of the EFCA is the last: the card-check system may *never* be used to displace an incumbent union, for EFCA explicitly applies only so long as "no other individual or labor organization is currently certified or recognized as the exclusive representative of any of the employees in the unit."[91] The implicit judgment is that card checks are too unreliable to displace a union, even though they are reliable enough to entrench one. The defenders of the statute give no explanation as to why this one-sided legal regime for recognition elections does not work in other

---

90. 29 U.S.C. 9(c)(B)(2).
91. EFCA, §2(a), modifying § 9(c) (29 U.S.C. 159 (c)).

contexts, given the ever-present risk of coercion in all contexts. But the political explanation for this skewed result is easy to identify. The EFCA only allows the card-check system that improves the odds of union representation. It rejects that approach where the card check would either reduce or transfer union representation.

Administrative Difficulties

The situation is even graver in light of the administrative difficulties in running a card-check system. The exact particulars of the new regime would have to be fleshed out by regulation or administrative process, adding yet another layer of uncertainty. In all likelihood the rules will make it difficult to resist a union petition for certification. In particular, either a card check or petition is likely to suffice as a serious statement of interest in union representation. Otherwise formal requirements for validity are nonexistent. Under EFCA, the union need not even have the employee's signature witnessed, for example, by a notary public to establish its validity. Because employees would have no way of knowing whether false or fraudulent authorization cards were submitted on their behalf, there is no way that a card-check system could replicate the reliability and freedom of expression provided by a secret ballot election.

Any card-check pattern is likely to follow the current NLRB hands-off practices, which give a firm little or no voice in determining card validity. Nor do existing state public bargaining statutes instill confidence that authorization card "validity" procedures would be effective. The Illinois Labor Relations Board (ILRB) routinely accepts any card that lists the name of the union along with some statement that acknowledges that the employee's signature should be regarded as evidence that the worker is willing to accept union representation in an appropriate bargaining unit. It does not appear that the particular contours of the unit need be stated on the signed card, even though their specification might influence the worker's choice. Rather, so long as the unit ultimately identified *after* the cards are collected meets the requirements of a suitable bargaining unit, the signature is binding. The union can wait to designate its bargaining unit until it sees the distribution of cards, at which point it will pick that unit that will maximize its gain. It is of course possible for a worker to limit that union discretion by indicating clearly on the card that he is only signing on for an election. Union organizers are not likely to present those cards after EFCA.

Once the cards are presented to the NLRB for certification, two activities will take place on parallel tracks. On the legal side, the parties will have to argue over the definition of the appropriate bargaining unit, which will be a challenging task for firms that are not unionized. There are no natural boundaries by location or occupation that leap out as decisive characteristics, and the parties will always jockey for position depending on the perceived distribution of the cards. The union, which will have a leg up in the dispute, will seek to define the largest unit over which it could command a majority, but will insist on a smaller unit if it cannot. Management will seek to steer the unit in the opposite direction. The validation process will become ever more complex if two or more unions are seeking certification, with some overlap in their expected membership, which could require either clever line-drawing or perhaps a Board-supervised election to resolve the matter. In the interim, uncertainty is likely to have a negative impact on firm performance. Costs become difficult to estimate, and some workers may look elsewhere for jobs or quit over their uneasiness in working in a union establishment.

The parallel issue is whether the signature cards or names are valid for the purposes of this act, where again the NLRB procedures give short shrift to independent employer objections. The Illinois experience with public unions is worth noting. Within seven days after the ILRB receives the majority interest (or MI) petition, the employer is obligated to provide both a list of the employees in the proposed bargaining unit and signature exemplars for those employees, including signatures on W-2 forms or other official documents. That list provided by the employer includes only those employees in the proposed bargaining unit as of the date the petition was filed. Quite possibly, the cards of former employees would count, even though they could not vote in an election after they departed. The only test of genuineness is a comparison of the two signatures by a Board agent who normally has no expertise in handwriting analysis. It could be difficult to detect some forgeries with this device. The system is surely less reliable than requiring the worker to appear before a neutral party to sign a card that could then become the specimen for comparison, where only those signatures that match count.

The limited nature of the employer's challenge to card validity also matters. The inquiry into validity is focused only on the narrow question of whether the card was signed by the worker within six months—or one year in NLRB proceedings—before the petition was signed. The system does not offer the employer any effective way to challenge the cards on the ground that the signature date has been altered, for the workers are not required to file a duplicate in any lockbox which can be dated as of the time of their arrival, ready for use if the union files the petition. Nor is there any requirement of notarization. As noted above, a worker is not allowed to withdraw the card before the appointed date. The decision not to count a card depends on the proof in the individual case, by "clear and convincing evidence of fraud." This tough standard is not met under current law by referring to the background risk that unions will engage in coercive tactics to win an election. Yet neither employer nor dissenting workers are allowed to take depositions of the card signatories to gather information about any violation. Nor does it appear that individual workers may come forward on their own to testify that they had been tricked into joining a union.

Faced with these limitations, it is highly unlikely that an employer could carry the burden of proving coercion by the "clear and convincing evidence" needed to reject the card check result. It is not surprising that there is no reported instance of setting aside any card check under the fraud and coercion provisions of the Illinois Labor Relations Act. The entire system is out of whack. In a close dispute, one or two votes could make all the difference. But under EFCA, all errors in administration skew the outcome in favor of the union. As the risk of fraud goes up with the card check, the level of administrative and judicial oversight goes down. The situation will only get worse if the level of card-check activity increases after EFCA. Yet the entire statute contains no provisions to deal with the huge volume of dispute and litigation that the provision will raise. The bottom line is that the introduction of the card-check system is precipitous and unwise. The current law on this point is not, and cannot be, perfect. But it is vastly superior to the card-check system that EFCA proposes to substitute in its place.

CHAPTER 2

MANDATORY ARBITRATION OF
TERMS AND RESTRICTIONS

NO MODEST PROPOSAL

To date, the card-check provisions have grabbed most of the
headlines in the debate over EFCA. Its most dramatic
departure from sound practice lies, in my view, in its cate-
gorical insistence on interest arbitration. "Interest arbitration" is a
term used in opposition to "grievance arbitration," which governs
disputes that arise under the underlying contractual provisions that
are already in place. As the Supreme Court stated nearly fifty years
ago in the *Steelworkers Trilogy*, grievance arbitration affords an
enormous scope to arbitrators to resolve disputes in accordance
with the terms and surrounding circumstances of a given contract.[1]
It is not the role of grievance arbitrators to impose their own views

---

1. *See, e.g.*, United Steelworkers of America v. American Mfg. Co., 363 U.S. 564 (1960);
United Steelworkers of America v. Warrior & Gulf Navigation Co., 363 U.S. 574 (1960);
For judicial deference to arbitration, *see* United Steelworkers of America v. American Manufacturing Co., 363 U.S. 564, (1960): "The function of a court is very limited when the
parties have agreed to submit all questions of contract interpretation to the arbitrator." *See
also*, United Steelworkers of America v. Warrior & Gulf Navigation Co., 363 U.S. 574
(1960), "The collective bargaining agreement states the rights and duties of the parties. It
is more than a contract; it is a generalized code to govern a myriad of cases which the
draftsmen cannot wholly anticipate." United Steelworkers of America v. Enterprise
Wheel & Car Corp., 363 U.S. 593 (1960). *See* for praise of arbitration, Harry Shulman,
Reason, Contract, and Law in Labor Relations, 68 Harv. L. Rev. 999, 1024 (1955), cited in
Warrior & Gulf: Arbitration "is a means of making collective bargaining work and thus
preserving private enterprise in a free government."

on management or labor, but to gather information from the express terms of the contract and "from the common law of the shop."[2] Written text and common practice under the agreement are the hallmarks of grievance arbitration. The Supreme Court has held that courts should give enormous deference to arbitrators on all matters of law and fact arising out of grievance arbitration.

Interest arbitration is a very different process. As the term suggests, the purpose of an arbitrator is to determine the "interests" of both parties to the agreement. The new arbitral role is to set the terms of the agreement, not to interpret or apply a pre-existing arrangement. In some instances, interest arbitration is done through mutual agreement. Under EFCA it is done pursuant to statutory mandate over the objection of the employer. Either way, of course, the level of discretion afforded to the arbitrator is far greater than with respect to grievances. I shall discuss later the legal implications of the two forms of arbitration. For the moment, it suffices to note the sweeping changes wrought by EFCA. Its arbitral process leads to a first "contract"—the word must be put in quotation marks—under which a panel of arbitrators, chosen by an as-yet-unknown process, imposes whatever terms it deems fit for a two-year period, without possibility of judicial review. This innovation marks a complete departure from the current law which provides that once a union has been certified, both the union and the employer fall under an obligation to bargain in good faith. In those cases in which neither side commits a ULP, a bargaining impasse imposes no obligation on either side to cooperate with the other. A union could order a strike and an employer could conduct a lock-out of union workers and hire replacement workers who keep their positions as long as the strike endures, and perhaps gain some protection once the strike is concluded.[3] These prospects are not all

---

2. Warrior & Gulf, 363 U.S. at 582.

3. NLRB v. Mackay Radio & Telegraph Co., 304 U.S. 333 (1938), allowing replacements when the employer has taken a strike in the absence of any ULP. In some instances, however, striking workers may have priority over new applicants for jobs at the conclusion of the strike. *See* NLRB v. Fleetwood Trailer, Cos, 389 U.S. 375 (1967).

that attractive to any business large or small, and the willingness of an employer to take a tough stance in negotiation is best understood as a measure of how much it thinks it will lose in operating flexibility, wages, and competitive position under a collective bargaining contract.

The relative calculus is changed even if compulsory arbitration is grafted onto a system of labor law that retains union elections. Once the union is so selected, the EFCA's three-step process, lasting 130 days, would still kick in, except when the parties accept extensions by mutual agreement. The union can, at the expiration of this 130-day period, force the employer's hand, for at that time, "the [Federal Mediation and Conciliation] Service shall refer the dispute to an arbitration board established in accordance with such regulations as may be prescribed by the Service. The arbitration panel shall render a decision settling the dispute and such decision shall be binding upon the parties for a period of two years, unless amended during such period by written consent of the parties."[4] Thus, the most radical transformation in American labor law is brought about in two sentences. But on the particulars of this novel program there is only silence. The only point the EFCA resolves is that arbitration is before either a "board" or a "panel," which presumably contains three members, perhaps more. But it is no easy matter to deploy compulsory arbitration to fill in the blanks on an empty piece of paper, and the gaps in EFCA left to regulation are legion and the consequences momentous.

A fundamental issue that EFCA does not address at all is: how should the statutory obligation to negotiate in good faith cash out in a legal environment where neither party has the option to walk away from the negotiations? The current framework states that the statute "does not compel either party to agree to a proposal or require the making of a concession."[5] The billion-dollar question

4. S. 1041, § 3, adding section 8(h) to 29 U.S.C. § 158.
5. Section 8(d), 29 U.S.C. § 158(d).

is whether this provision remains operative within a compulsory arbitration regime. Here, in principle, the most sensible approach under EFCA's unsound institutional framework is to dispense with good-faith bargaining requirements altogether. Intransigence no longer has any real benefits given that the arbitral panel can structure its decree to sanction an obstructionist party. If one side refuses to cooperate, the other party just runs out the clock and the matter goes straight to arbitration after 130 days where time limits can be enforced. As part of that process the panel can decide how to apportion blame as it fashions its decree. The rest of the bad-faith apparatus can be ignored because EFCA's more draconian methods have effectively made it futile to refuse to bargain. The overall change in the NLRA should lead to a complete recalibration of the entire statute. EFCA of course does not take this approach. Instead it leaves open the question of how its compulsory arbitration scheme meshes with the current set of duties to bargain in good faith. Here are some of the difficulties.

TRANSITIONAL PROVISIONS

The initial shortcoming in this approach to compulsory arbitration is that no steps were made to insure an orderly transition or to issue regulations that could answer the question just posed on the proper integration of EFCA with existing institutions. Rather, the Act calls for the law to take effect immediately on passage. EFCA contains no provision that delays the effective date of the statute to allow the various government agencies to finalize the regulations that are supposed to govern its operation. That shortcoming may not be too acute with respect to the card-check provision because the existing systems already in place answer, however unsatisfactorily, the key questions on implementation. But the same optimistic estimation cannot be made of the interest arbitration provisions that promise a radical alteration in the form of labor negotiations.

As will become clear, the gaps take place at each stage of the process, yet the total absence of guidance leaves everyone ill-equipped to deal with the multiple contingencies that are sure to crop up in negotiations that will be fraught with tension from the outset. Major statutes such as the Civil Rights Act of 1964 contained provisions that delayed their implementation for a year in order to allow parties to follow the basic procedures of the Administrative Procedure Act with respect to the promulgation of key regulations.[6]

INITIATION OF BARGAINING

The problems of integrating EFCA's compulsory arbitration system with the NLRA's obligation to bargain in good faith begin with the first procedural step. It is extraordinarily difficult to get any negotiations off the ground within ten days after the recognition of a union if both parties are to comply with the basic mechanics of bargaining under the NLRA. And the result of union certification via a card check will set the stage for precipitous negotiations. But notwithstanding the likely distrust on both sides, the work must continue. This is no easy task. Over the past six decades, an extensive body of NLRB law provides that the obligation to bargain not only includes meeting at "reasonable times," but also the disclosure of information reasonably necessary for the parties to discharge their respective obligations to bargain in good faith.[7] In practice, the standard union requests for troves of information typically precipitate disputes over the form and manner by which relevant data is turned over to the union, the appropriate treatment of confidential information, the financial capabilities of the employer to meet pay demands, and the allocation of the costs incurred in turning over, subject to safeguards, certain types of sensitive information.

---

6. Civil Rights Act of 1964 ETC date of implementation section. Administrative Procedure Act, 5 U.S.C. §§500 et seq.

7. Section 8(d), 29 U.S.C. § 158(d).

A ten-day period does not permit an adequate resolution of issues surrounding the assembly, preservation, and transfer of information in the heated context of negotiations. Yet EFCA contains no provisions that indicate what adjustments, if any, should be made in the bargaining schedule when these negotiations are unable to begin on time. Nor does it contain any indication of whether either side, or both, will be viewed as having committed a ULP when and if the negotiations break down. Is the NLRB going to have to make determinations of which side failed to cooperate, when both may have dragged their feet? And what schedule will the negotiations take while any such determination is made? It may be sufficient for popular consumption to state that the statutory timetable should be faithfully followed. But it is critical for any successful system to put in place a detailed decision tree that sets out the procedures to be applied and the consequences of failure to meet the deadlines at each stage of the process. These gaps in the timetable are sure to provoke further dislocations in the subsequent stages of the process, which in turn will be the source of further disputes.

Negotiation and Mediation

The initial difficulties on integration are likely to be compounded during the continuous process of negotiation and mediation. There are countless reasons, both good and bad, why parties may be unable to keep to the tight schedules set out under EFCA. It is common for members of high-profile negotiation teams to face crises in other areas of their business, to deal with other EFCA negotiations, to get sick, or to take leave for family emergencies. Multiple commitments and logistical difficulties, like storms and floods, could easily throw negotiations off schedule. The possibilities for confusion become greater during the mediation stage of negotiations, for EFCA contains no provisions that indicate what should

be done if the mediator fails to show up as scheduled. These difficulties could be addressed by informal adjustments of the schedule
by mutual consent. But so long as either side has some strategic
advantage from insisting on expediting the process, there are no
guarantees that these ongoing modifications will be implemented,
and no indication of what dispute mechanisms are appropriate in
the event of breakdown. Even if the obvious question of how arbitration should proceed when one side claims that mediation has
not run its course is left unanswered by the statute.

EFCA also fails to integrate its own rapid timetables with the
traditional enforcement machinery under the NLRA that works
under a different clock. For more than sixty years, the NLRA has
required both the union and the employer to engage in "good-
faith" bargaining.[8] It is unclear how these obligations would be
recast under EFCA. On one track, EFCA drives any unresolved
agreement into mandatory arbitration after 120 days. On a second
track, disputes over whether either side has engaged in bad-faith
bargaining can easily linger, because both sides may petition the
NLRB for up to six months after the occurrence of the alleged misconduct.[9] The upshot is that a barrage of ULP claims could intersect
with a prolonged arbitration process, lending uncertainty to both
regimes.

Nor will the difficulties quickly disappear. Filing of a ULP charge
represents only the first step of a complex process. Historically,
most bad faith bargaining cases take time to work their way
through different appellate levels. Some important cases might not
reach the five-member NLRB for years. But what happens to the
Board's efforts to impose remedies on an employer or union which
it finds has bargained in bad faith during the 120-day bargaining
period preceding mandatory arbitration? How can the NLRB devise
a meaningful remedy when, in the interim, a panel of arbitrators

8. Sections 8(a)(5), 8(b)(3), 8(d), 29 U.S.C. §§ 158(a)(5), 8(b)(3), 8(d).
9. NLRA § 10(b), 29 U.S.C. § 160(b).

has forced an arrangement upon the parties for the two-year period prescribed under EFCA? Ironically, if a useful remedy is no longer possible, EFCA effectively undercuts the NLRA's requirement of good-faith bargaining in relation to initial agreements.

Alternatively, EFCA may result in an enormous number of NLRB-adjudicated bad-faith bargaining disputes. Think of the complications just on the wage issues. If the employer's conduct is thought to be improper, does that lead to retroactive wage increases, including ones that apply *after* the conclusion of the initial two-year period? Alternatively, if a union is found to have violated its good-faith bargaining obligations, after an EFCA-empowered arbitration panel has awarded it a favorable wage rate, should anything be done to unravel the gains that the arbitrator has improperly bestowed on union membership? Does that form of intervention apply only to wage terms or to other aspects of the initial arbitral decree, some of which could have hurt the firm financially or even driven it into bankruptcy? It would be most unfortunate if any of these scenarios were to make a mockery of the "certainty beforehand" to which the United States Supreme Court gives pride of place when applying the NLRA to fundamental business changes.[10]

COMPULSORY INTEREST ARBITRATION

A Standard-less Process

The greatest difficulties under EFCA arise with its most daring innovation: the use of mandatory arbitration to resolve all contract disputes. At this coercive stage of the proceeding, it becomes critical to set out the rules by which both parties will be bound. Yet once again EFCA opts for one broad mandate with no details. Nothing in the statute settles questions of how arbitration panels are to be

---

10. First National Maintenance Corp. v. NLRB, 452 U.S. 666, 678–79 (1981).

set up, the scope of their powers, or the reviewability of their decrees on matters of fact and law. Nor does EFCA make any effort to indicate the set of relevant considerations for the arbitral decrees, and in this regard is in sharp contrast with the detailed specifications of procedures and standards found in many state laws that require interest arbitration in the public sector.[11]

The catalog of unresolved questions prior to arbitration is very large, especially for firms with no history of union relationships. There is, moreover, nothing in EFCA that questions the validity of checked cards collected before passage of the Act, so that the NLRB could easily be inundated with cases right after its passage. One hundred and thirty days is an exceedingly tight time frame, not only for negotiations but also for the entire notice and comment proceeding that the NLRB and the FMCS will have to complete in order to put the bill into action. The failure to establish any standards before the organization drives begin could easily overwhelm the agency and lead to inconsistent patterns in individual cases. Some delay before implementation is needed no matter what view is taken on the desirability of the so-called "reforms."

Structure of the Arbitration Panels

On matters of procedure, the first question involves the selection of the arbitration panel. Many arbitration panels consist of three persons, one of whom is selected by each party, after which the two arbitrators select the third, or neutral, arbitrator. This selection process may be made more complex. For example, each side may first present a slate of potential arbitrators. Thereafter the other side may be able to veto some number of those choices or, less likely,

---

11. Illinois Public Labor Relations Act, 5 ILCS 315 5/1 *et seq.* (2008). Section 9(a-5) establishes certification of exclusive bargaining representatives pursuant to "card check"; and Section 14 sets forth the interest arbitration process in the public sector.

select the arbitrator from the opposing list that it finds most desirable. But there is no necessity for the FMCS to follow these patterns when it issues its regulations.

In principle, the FMCS could appoint all three members of the arbitration panel by itself. For all the statute provides, it could pick all three (or more) arbitrators exclusively from the ranks of labor or management, which raises a question of bias of constitutional magnitude—one that should prompt a strong procedural due process claim under the Fifth Amendment to the United States Constitution. More likely, the FMCS will promulgate regulations that will give each side some control over the selection of at least one arbitrator. But that approach does nothing to resolve the impasse that will arise over the appointment of the critical third arbitrator with his tie-breaking role. Here the FMCS will have to take an active hand. But so long as it is subject to political influence—which seems inevitable—it is likely to pick a decisive arbitrator who is temperamentally in favor of one side or the other. Whether the regulations will allow any administrative or judicial challenges to the arbitral selection, it is not possible to say. Nor is it clear that the decision of the Board with such adversarial consequences will be entitled to administrative deference under the *Chevron* doctrine.[12] The claims for expertise are thin in this context and the risk of obvious bias in the selection of any "neutral" arbitrator is clear.

Powers of the Arbitration Panels

Once the panel is selected, what is the scope of the arbitration, and how will the panel gain the information to flesh out the first nonconsensual decree? The current law tends to afford unions broad, but not unlimited, discretion in framing the requests for

---

12. Chevron U.S.A. Inc., v. Natural Resources Defense Council, Inc., 467 U.S. 837 (1984).

information that they serve on employers. I have already commented on how unlikely it is that these matters could be resolved within a ten-day period. But it should not be assumed that these common problems exclude another set of issues that is more likely to crop up in a first-round negotiation between two parties with no common history of negotiations. The discretion to request information is broad but it is not unlimited. There are some matters that an employer may shield from a union, and claims of this type of privilege could be exceptionally difficult to resolve in some arbitration proceedings.

Information is a valuable commodity. One serious issue is whether its release carries with it improper use or transmission to third parties. To guard against these risks the obligation to disclose in a union context is typically limited for two reasons. First, the union typically has no information of value that it could release to the employer, so all these disclosures must run in one direction—to the union. Second, the courts have a real uneasiness about allowing open-ended requests for information. In *NLRB v. Truitt Manufacturing*,[13] the Supreme Court affirmed the long-standing Board position that good-faith negotiations required the employer to back up its claims to be unable to grant workers a ten-cent-per-hour increase by disclosing sufficient financial information to the union. The Court limited that obligation, however, to inquiries that were not "unduly burdensome or injurious to its business."[14] More critically, in *Detroit Edison v. NLRB*,[15] the court refused to order the defendant utility to disclose the particulars of psychological tests to determine whether its promotions were in conformity with a collective bargaining agreement which allowed seniority to be displaced only when "the reasonable qualifications and abilities of the employees being considered are not significantly different."[16]

---

13. 351 U.S. 149 (1956).
14. *Id.* at 151.
15. 440 U.S. 301 (1979).
16. *Id.*

The range of relevant information is broader under interest arbitration than under grievance arbitration, so these trade-secret-versus-disclosure conflicts will be more frequent and more acute. Within this new context, it is unclear what information should count as burdensome under *Truitt* or confidential under *Detroit Edison*. It takes no imagination, however, to conclude that an arbitration panel could routinely require the employer to disclose to the union extensive information about many aspects of the employer's activities as part of the comprehensive arbitration process. That information will in all likelihood cover job classifications and wages, pension and benefit information for all workers within the unit, all of which are mandatory subjects of negotiation.[17] This information, which contains valuable clues as to the employer's business plan, would normally count as a trade secret.[18] Nor is it likely under EFCA that the employer could resist demands made under subpoena about salary information for nonunion workers in the firm in order to establish ostensible standards of comparability.

Given the scope of this mandatory arbitration, financial and salary information might be only the start. Work rules, promotion and discipline policy, sick leave, and disability are all mandatory matters that must be addressed in current collective bargaining negotiations. They are, therefore, proper matters before the EFCA's arbitral panel. Some portion of that information may be already available in employee handbooks, but those publications would not contain internal management estimates of cost or protocols for implementation that could be subject to discovery. Many small businesses are in the process of rapid growth, which makes the release of any information about their expansion plans of great value to competitors. The release of their information could reduce

---

17. *See* Inland Steel Co. v. NLRB, 179 F.2d 247, 251 (7th Cir. 1948).

18. *See* Restatement (Third) of Unfair Competition § 39 (1995): "A trade secret is any information that can be used in the operation of a business or other enterprise and that is sufficiently valuable and secret to afford an actual or potential economic advantage over others."

their prospects for going public or for being bought out by some larger firm.

At the other end of the spectrum, most complex businesses have elaborate procedures for work done within the firm and work contracted out to other parties, including the details of all outsourcing contracts on work that the union would likely want to reclaim for the bargaining unit, perhaps to determine potential liabilities for contractual breach. Large firms constantly acquire new businesses and shed old ones, so all the thorny questions of successor liability also will be brought into the arbitration process. The standard private sector collective bargaining agreement for small units can run to hundreds of pages on dozens of different topics. The sparse words of EFCA give no hint of how the arbitrators will collect and interpret the information needed for the system of interest arbitration. Failing agreement, disputed matters may yet wind up in further litigation. But EFCA is silent on internal appeals within the FMCS or by interlocutory appeals to courts.

Scope of Compulsory Arbitration

EFCA is also silent on the topics covered by its proposed arbitration scheme. Under section 8(d) of the NLRA, the obligation for good-faith negotiation extends to "wages, hours, and other terms and conditions of employment."[19] The first two terms are relatively clear, but the phrase "other terms and conditions of employment" is highly elastic. The House version of section 8(d) contained a long list of topics to which the duty to bargain would attach:

> (i) wage rates, hours of employment, and work requirements; (ii) procedures and practices relating to discharge, suspension, lay-off, recall, seniority, and discipline, or to promotion, demotion, transfer and assignment within the bargaining unit; (iii) conditions, procedures, and practices, governing safety, sanitation, and protection of

19. Section 8(d); 29 U.S.C. §158(d).

health at the place of employment; (iv) vacations and leaves of absence; and (v) administrative and procedural provisions relating to the foregoing subjects.[20]

Which of these topics is covered by the more general phrase "other terms and conditions of employment," is a matter of some dispute over such key questions as furloughs and reduction-in-force arrangements. Those disagreements are surely important under the current system, but they are not life-and-death matters given that either side can simply refuse to budge on those issues that it regards as critical. But the classification of any of these issues as mandatory under EFCA is truly transformative, because once the subject is raised the arbitral panel is not bound to follow any common practice whereby firms refuse to yield control over these matters to the union under the collective bargaining agreement. The absence of any guidance as to the limits of the arbitral power is yet another of the major structural weaknesses in EFCA.

To make matters more difficult, the existing case law draws an elusive but critical distinction between mandatory and permissive terms of bargaining. As to the former, both sides are required to seek some honest agreement. Nonetheless, each side is allowed to propose that an agreement on mandatory terms be achieved by adding other "permissive" terms into the agreement. These permissive terms are those that either party can put forward, but on which neither side can insist if the other side refuses to include them in the negotiations. Matters of product design, advertising, new stock issues, and credit arrangements fall clearly outside the scope of mandatory bargaining. But as matters get closer to the workplace environment, the line-drawing becomes more difficult. One example of a permissive term, for example, is an employer's demand to a union that an employer's last offer be put to a vote of unit members before the union may call a strike.[21]

---

20. As quoted in Robert A. Gorman & Matthew W. Finkin, *Basic Text on Labor Law, Unionization and Collective Bargaining* 673 (West Publishing Co. 2004).

21. *See* NLRB v. Wooster Division of Borg-Warner Corp., 356 U.S. 342 (1958).

Speaking generally, EFCA does not state in so many words whether any permissive terms could be made subject to a mandatory system of "first contract" arbitration. On one view, mandatory arbitration should mimic any agreement that the parties themselves would reach. Since voluntary agreements include permissive topics of negotiation, these then become subject to arbitral consideration like any other—at which point either side could expand the list of topics relevant to arbitration. In principle, however, the better view limits the coercive arbitral arrangement to mandatory terms only. A matter that could not be forced into traditional negotiations should not be made part of the final coercive decree unless both parties consent. Unfortunately, like so many issues under EFCA, the point is left hanging.

Under *Fibreboard Paper Products Corp. v. NLRB*, the list of mandatory collective bargaining issues includes a wide range of issues relating to the size of the workforce.[22] One such provision is the so-called management rights clause, which in general terms preserves to management the right to retain its "normal prerogatives" in the operation of the firm's business, which the Supreme Court has held management may insist on in good faith.[23] Often these clauses specify in great detail the types of decisions that fall exclusively to management during the course of the contract. In principle, an arbitrator could conclude that no decision relating to the introduction of new products or the modes of production, or even the price of goods, could be done without union approval. These examples are not fancy extensions of *Fibreboard,* which treated as a mandatory bargaining issue any "contracting out" of work for the business that could be performed by unit members to third persons. More specifically, *Fibreboard* held that a decision by an employer to contract out its maintenance operations to third persons was a subject of mandatory bargaining because it took work away from current unit members.

22. 379 U.S. 203 (1964).
23. NLRB v. American National Insurance Co., 343 U.S. 395 (1952).

This subject is exceedingly important. For arbitral decisions to prevent contracting out of any work by a single unit in the firm could easily make it difficult to retain flexibility in work assignments for nonunion workers elsewhere in the firm. Let the firm have an integrated process in which it only makes sense to contract out an entire job; then an arbitral decree with respect to a single union will dictate policy for the treatment of nonunion work. But *Fibreboard's* reach remains, even today, somewhat unclear because the Court also noted that "[o]ur decision need not and does not encompass other forms of 'contracting out' or 'subcontracting' which arise daily in our complex economy."

That disclaimer does not indicate just how far this duty to bargain runs. In *First National Maintenance Corp. v. NLRB*,[24] the Court held that the employer had no duty to bargain over the decision to shut down a part of its business by canceling particular contracts. But *First National* does not undermine *Fiberboard's* central proposition that mandatory bargaining can cover many decisions about subcontracting out unit work. Nor does it resolve all the questions about whether there is a duty to bargain over such key questions as whether a firm may relocate all or part of its operations from one facility to another. That issue is not one which is amenable to clear delineation. The NLRB formulation of the question in *Dubuque Packing Co.*[25] makes the question turn on the differences in the operations and the two locations and the motivations for moving from one place to another. Under *Dubuque* it is open for an employer to prove by a preponderance of the evidence "(1) that labor costs (direct or indirect) were not a factor in the decision, or (2) that even if labor costs were a factor in the decision, the union could not have offered labor cost concession that could have changed the employer's decision to relocate."[26] I quote this language from the NLRB

24. 452 U.S. 666 (1981).

25. 303 NLRB 386 (1991), enforced UFCA, Local 150-A v. NLRB (Dubuque Packing Co., 1 F.3d 24 (D.C. Cir. 1993). *Dubuque* was not followed in Dorsey Trailers, Inc. v. NLRB, 233 F.3d 831 (4th Cir. 2000).

26. 303 NLRB at 391.

because it shows just how difficult it is to decide matters of mandatory bargaining even after a full record of the transaction becomes available. It seems the case that none of this information will be easily assembled in the interest arbitration proceedings under EFCA. An arbitration panel may believe it is empowered to prevent the outsourcing of further work, to block the relocation of business facilities, or even to bring back in-house work that had been outsourced. It is unclear whether these extraordinary restrictions, never agreed to by the employer, would properly fall within the scope of the arbitral decree. Nor is it clear whether the final arbitration could require the employer to terminate or abrogate existing contracts with third parties as inconsistent with the collective bargaining agreement and, if so, whether the decree would shield the employer from an action for contract damages or perhaps even specific performance. All that is known is that it has long been held that a collective bargaining agreement abrogates prior individual contracts that an employer made with unit members before the selection of the union as the bargaining agent.[27] How this plays out with other agreements remains a mystery. For large and complex businesses, literally hundreds of these third-party agreements could be exposed to arbitral review, when their invalidation or modification could pose serious issues of third-party liability.

This same risk could occur with the pension rights of workers within the unit. Pension plans for existing (but not future) employees are a mandatory topic of negotiation.[28] It therefore seems likely that the arbitrator could impose on the company a variety of provisions that modify pension benefits for current unit members, raising thorny questions of which benefits under the pension plan are vested in the employees. Among the intriguing possibilities are orders that the employer make contributions to some multiemployer plan, even one which is underfunded, so that the firm

---

27. *See* J.I. Case. Co. v. NLRB, 321 U.S. 332 (1944).
28. Allied Chemical Workers Local 1 v. Pittsburgh Plate Glass Co., 404 U.S. 157 (1971).

suffers in expectation a net loss from joining in that venture. Any such decision could generate enormous liabilities for the employer if, for example, it subsequently experiences changes that constitute a "withdrawal" from the multi-employer pension plan.[29] The obvious question is whether the dictation of these rights constitutes a confiscation of the property interests of either employers or unions, which will require extensive and time-consuming litigation to settle. For the moment it is simply enough to note the enormous reach of arbitral power. These examples can be easily multiplied, because nothing limits the scope of that arbitration.

Interest Arbitration Extensions?

Another critical question concerns the simple issue of whether the initial arbitral decree could stipulate that the next contract negotiation—and the next after that—could be subject to the EFCA's mandatory arbitration provisions. Ideally, EFCA should have stated that it does not permit extensions but only applies to "first contract" arbitrations. In the absence of any real guidance on this question, it seems that this is the proper result. The key question under current law is whether one labor contract could stipulate that both sides accept interest arbitration for the negotiation of the extension of the original contract. That result would be proper if interest arbitration were a mandatory bargaining subject under current law. Yet the case law on this point seems to cut the opposite way. In *NLRB v. Columbus Printing Pressmen Union No. 252*,[30] the court found that it was a ULP under section 8(b)(3) for the union to insist that this clause be included in the next agreement. Its basic conclusion was that this clause fundamentally altered the nature of bargaining by removing the right to refuse to make concessions during the

---

29. *See* on these plans, Concrete Pipe & Products of California, Inc. v. Construction Laborers Pension Trust for Southern California, 508 U.S. 602 (1993).

30. 543 F.2d 1161 (5th Cir. 1976).

next period, especially since the union could insist on interest arbitration during the next period. The fear of a "self-perpetuating" interest arbitration scheme was key to this decision. That fear also drove the decision in *American Metal Products v. Sheet Metal Workers Local 104*, where the court refused to require a second round of interest-arbitration pursuant to an initial interest-arbitration award.[31] That result should apply a fortiori to any initial interest-arbitration award that EFCA imposes.

The situation under EFCA is still more complex because it is unclear what status should attach to an arbitral award that erroneously covers matters that are properly classified as permissive. On this question, current law has little to say about compulsory interest-arbitration, because it is so rare in the private sector. But when arbitration takes place pursuant to the agreement of the parties, the Supreme Court has taken a deferential approach that leaves the arbitration decisions undisturbed on appeal—of which none is allowed under EFCA—even when the arbitrators have committed "grievous error" or made "improvident, even silly fact-finding."[32] That approach may make sense in light of the long tradition that affords extraordinary deference to grievance arbitration chosen by the parties.[33] But it hardly makes sense with respect to coercive arbitration done without judicial review, except perhaps in bankruptcy, where all too many of these cases are likely to land. The fact that on many topics—e.g., subcontracting and relocation—the line between mandatory and permissive bargaining may depend on subjective factors and negotiation behavior puts incredible burdens on a system. Once again, the constitutional specter of due process violations appears to loom large against EFCA, which contains no safeguards at all against arbitral misbehavior. Even the strongest supporters of interest arbitration must acknowledge that the gaps

---

31. 794 F.2d 1452 (9th Cir. 1986).
32. United Paperworkers International Union v. Misco, 484 U.S. 29, 39 (1987).
33. *See* discussion of the *Steelworkers Trilogy, supra* note 1.

in EFCA render the scheme unworkable, especially if introduced on a mass basis at breakneck speed.

Right-to-Work Laws

Whatever the ambiguities elsewhere, EFCA's interest arbitration provision does not appear to preempt state right-to-work laws. Section 14(b) of the NLRA provides: "nothing in this Act shall be construed as authorizing the execution or application of agreements requiring membership in any State or Territory in which such execution or application is prohibited by State or Territorial law." This section allows individual states to outlaw so-called union security clauses, which usually take one of two forms. First, a "union shop" clause requires a worker to join a union, and thereby assume all the obligations of union membership, within a fixed period after the union has been recognized. The weaker "agency shop" provision only requires that the worker who chooses not to join a union be required to make some contribution to the union in lieu of dues. It does not appear, however, that interest arbitration could go any further in the future than voluntary negotiations could on this matter today. If conventional negotiations could not bind dissenting workers in right-to-work states, the same result should hold for interest arbitration under EFCA, just as it does for efforts to build an extension of EFCA in the original interest arbitration decree. One area of ambiguity remains, for nothing in EFCA precludes the arbitrator from setting stiff fees in agency shop jurisdiction, as an obvious deterrent to workers opting out of the unions.

ECONOMIC CONSEQUENCES OF INTEREST ARBITRATION

Administrative Costs

The implementation of any scheme of compulsory arbitration in labor disputes will increase costs and uncertainty in negotiations.

The precise incidence of these costs is difficult to determine. As an initial guess, both sides will be required to bear half the direct costs of the arbitration process, as well as their own private costs of pressing the arbitration forward. These costs would tend to impose special burdens on small firms, which have no experience on these matters and would have to staff up at breakneck speed to meet their obligations under EFCA. In addition, the proposal will generate social costs in the form of more extensive government infrastructure to support the new regulatory apparatus. The exact amount of these costs cannot be estimated in advance, but the number cannot be small on an initial or ongoing basis. What are the social gains that justify these public and private expenditures? It turns out that these are hard to identify. Defenders of compulsory interest arbitration point to two justifications. The first is that it generates a higher level of industrial peace by removing the lockout and the strike from any "first contract" negotiation. The second is that the program has worked well in both the public and private sector. Both of these claims are false.

Industrial Peace

True, interest arbitration removes the risk of strikes and lockouts during the negotiation of the initial contract. But the issue of industrial peace cannot be measured at a single point in time; it must be measured over the entire cycle under EFCA, from original card check through contract renewals after the expiration of the initial period. Two other stages are involved.

First are the initial negotiations. I have already indicated why there is good reason to think that the card-check system will lead to squabbles between unions and management over the definition of the bargaining unit and the validity of individual signature cards. Likewise, EFCA makes no provision for unions or companies—in connection with bargaining—to formulate, exchange, and respond to requests for information and documentation. These requests are regular fixtures in conventional negotiations, but never under an expedited timetable. They assume a still greater role in a new and untested bargaining relationship, where the stakes are higher and the anticipated levels of cooperation lower.

Yet in the face of these evident obstacles EFCA makes no allowance for letting the employer and the union resolve questions pertaining to such requests. Nor does the NLRB have authorization to make an investigation of charges that unions or employers may make about the failure of the other side to satisfy its obligations to bargain in good faith, which may survive for employers under sections 8(a)(5) and for unions under section 8(b)(3). It is also unclear whether the 130-day period for negotiation is on hold until these ULP claims are resolved. With the stakes this high and the law this unclear, neither side will be disposed to back down once a dispute arises. In addition, the parties always bargain in the shadow of the law.[34] As Anne Layne-Farrar notes in her study, "If a union expects a more favorable arrangement through arbitration than it is currently being offered by the employer, union organizers have a strong incentive to refuse all terms proffered by the firm, no matter whether they are reasonable or not."[35] There is no reason for it to take anything less. Employers could make the same calculations, once they are drawn into the system against their will. The likelihood of a voluntary agreement could easily go down under this system, which puts greater pressure on the still-unknown arbitration process. Given that the levels of uncertainty are high, unions in particular may have a strong incentive to hold out for a strike-it-rich settlement, especially if they think the decisive arbitrator is on their side.

---

34. *See,* Henry Farber and Harry Katz, Interest Arbitration, Outcomes, and the Incentive to Bargain, 33 Indus. & Lab. Rel. Rev. 55, 55–63 (1979), noting how the arbitral context "directly affects the terms of the negotiated agreement."

35. Anne Layne-Farrar, An Empirical Assessment of the Employee Free Choice Act: The Economic Implications 13 (2009)available at http://papers.SSRN.com/sol3/papers.cfm?abstract_id1353305.

Second are the arbitral uncertainties. During the initial period, the arbitrated contract could easily turn out to create many undesirable consequences not foreseen or understood during the initial arbitration. And of course there is no guarantee that the arbitral decree will be clear enough to cover all disputes. It too could be the subject of disagreement and controversy. The EFCA offers no mechanism for the employer to make any unilateral midcourse correction. Nor does it contain any mechanism to resolve honest disputes over the interpretation of its decrees. Yet both these issues will be of great importance, since the original arbitral decree is likely to miss the mark on many issues. At this point, the union could easily be in a strong hold-up position with respect to issues that could spell life or death to the firm. But there appears no way for the arbitrators who made the initial mistake to correct the mistake on application of the employer. Similar issues could also arise in the opposite direction with respect to union activities. The extent of those mistakes, however, appears far smaller, as most of the arbitral provisions are likely to place sharp restrictions on management, and not union, prerogatives.

Third is the effective contract period. The issuance of an arbitration award does not end the cycle of disagreement. At the end of the two-year period, new ruptures will arise. For starters, EFCA states that the arbitration panel's decision "shall be binding upon the parties for a period of two years. . . ."[36] This does not make it clear whether the arbitral award is effective only from the date it is handed down, so that the previous business arrangements apply to the period between recognition and arbitration, or whether the two-year period will be retroactive, thereby making changes in wages or benefits binding from the date of union recognition. If the latter, prolonged arbitration could result in a decree whose effect could lapse just as it is announced, plunging the parties into a new

36. Employee Free Choice Act of 2007, H.R. 800, 110th Cong. § 3 (2007).

round of bargaining under traditional rules. Normally, the renegotiation of a collective bargaining agreement is a painful affair, especially if matters have not worked out well during the initial contract
period. Unions can press for objectives that they did not achieve at
the original stage, just as management can demand givebacks if
market conditions have become more competitive. Conversely, if
the two-year period runs from when the initial agreement dispute
is resolved, it necessarily follows that the initial decree would last
for a far longer period, during which it is unknown whether
employers and employees will be bound by pre-existing employment terms and conditions or by those imposed by the arbitration
panel. The duration of the arbitration proceedings would therefore
increase the hardship from the new terms dictated by the arbitral
process. It would also increase the possibility that both sides would
resort to conventional economic weapons, including strikes and
lockouts.

These familiar difficulties are certain to be magnified because the
basic arrangement is now the product of an imposed settlement
and not a voluntary agreement. At this point one side—probably
both management and disgruntled workers had no say in the initial
arbitration—will think that the entire previous arrangement has no
legitimacy because it was dictated by third-party arbitrators. The
upshot is that both critical stages in the life of a labor agreement
take place with no input from the employees who are forced to live
with the arrangement. They must first live with the denial of the
secret ballot that selects the union. Thereafter they have to live
under a contract whose terms they do not know, and whose provisions they do not have the opportunity to accept or reject. Freed
from the shackles of the original agreement, the management team
will bargain hard with the union in order to take back what it
regards as unacceptable arbitral fiats. It is therefore likely that the
pent-up antagonisms of a dictated regime will boil over. The ostensible peace when the "first contract" is imposed will be offset by
the increased tensions at other points in the negotiation cycle.

What Counts as Successful Arbitrations?

In order for any relationship to remain stable, it must leave each party better off than it would have been in the absence of the agreement. That condition can be satisfied, albeit with difficulty, in voluntary agreements between the two sides, for neither management nor labor will agree to any contract that leaves it worse off than it would have been with a lockout or a strike. But there is no guarantee that any complex arbitrator-imposed terms and restrictions under EFCA will meet this condition. Remember, the dispute here is not limited to salaries and benefits, but necessarily spills over to all terms that are part of a standard collective bargaining agreement. Many of these are not easy to monetize, such as work rules, promotions, demotions, reassignments, layoffs, grievances, and the like. Each of these provisions is hard to value, and it is easy for an arbitrator to underestimate the level of dislocation that a particular restriction will have on the competitive mettle of the firm.

The problem is even more difficult than it first appears for two reasons. The first relates to a single arbitral award: the many close interconnections between the various aspects of the employment relationship could impose unexpected burdens on the management of the firm. The problem is equally acute for small businesses and large ones. Two years is an eternity for any firm shackled with a labor agreement that makes it impossible to respond quickly to new dangers or opportunities. The implicit static model behind EFCA is at least a generation behind the times. The second relates to the prospect of multiple arbitral awards on behalf of different bargaining units in the same firm; there may be inconsistencies between the awards, or the cumulative burdens could easily escape the detection of the separate arbitration panels as they move along parallel tracks.

EFCA proponents insist these points are overstated because of the common use of these arrangements in the public sector, where neither strikes nor lockouts are allowed. But there are significant differences between public and private settings. Most public unions—teachers, police, firefighters, sanitation workers, and so on—work for a given public employer with a fixed internal structure that faces no direct competition from any other firm. There is, therefore, a certain forgiveness in the setting of terms because the government unit has the opportunity to make up any losses from contracts through increased taxes. In addition, contract renewals and extensions are typically negotiated off past agreements, which have already proved viable.

Viable, however, is far from optimal. With public employment, many of the terms are dictated by statute or regulation, which could easily be ill-suited for many bargaining units. Unfortunately, the parties have no opportunity to revise the basic agreement to counter any inefficiencies that arise. The basic contract structure lives on long after the efficient modes of production have shifted. The continuation in service may prevent disruptions, but it conceals the rapid deterioration that interest arbitration fosters by entrenching older modes of doing business in the face of new technology. The rubber hits the road whenever public institutions are faced with new competition. Methods of education and financing in public schools change slowly. Yet once a charter school is allowed to bid for students, the inefficiencies of the public system become apparent. It can adopt, for example, efficient backroom systems that will free up more resources for teaching. It can make innovations without having to clear a top-heavy bureaucracy. Hence we see the fierce opposition of teachers' unions to vouchers, charter schools, and home schooling for what they reveal about their own rigid organizational structure.[37] Efficient institutions do not have to fear new entrants whose cost structure is higher than their own. Inefficient institutions must drive out these new entrants by legal compulsion. Otherwise, parents will educate their children elsewhere. Interest arbitration by legal compulsion works only in sheltered environments.

---

37. *See, e.g.*, Milton Friedman, Public Schools: Make Them Private, Wash. Post, Feb. 19, 1997, at C7, available at http://www.heritage.org/Research/Education/ednotes96.cfm.

Private firms, of course, rarely enjoy the luxury of a state monopoly. They cannot keep out rivals that are more efficient. Interest arbitration can thus deal a fatal blow to any firm caught in its clutches. In the simplest situation, one firm is subject to a compulsory arbitration decree before its key rivals are unionized. Its labor bill goes up, its managerial flexibility goes down. The firm will face immediate losses that can be chalked up exclusively to the interest arbitration. There are countless variations on this theme, for even if two rival businesses are both subject to interest arbitration, their competitive balance could be profoundly shifted if the one arbitral decree imposes more onerous obligations on employer A than a second arbitral decree imposes on employer B.

Disparities will be everyday occurrences in these novel settings, especially for firms that have never been unionized. The arbitration panel has no template agreement on which to base its final decree. It operates largely in the dark, being able to rely at most on filtered information without any real appreciation for how a complex business operates. The leaps of faith are much greater, which means that the relative disparities between any two competitive firms will be far greater. But unlike the public sector, there is no monopoly protection to shield the blow.

Nor does the limited presence of voluntary interest arbitration in the private sphere indicate the contrary. These arbitration arrangements have been agreed to in advance by parties who have negotiated under the current rules governing collective bargaining. For example, based on unique circumstances then existing in the steel industry, the United Steelworkers and major steel industry producers in the early 1970s agreed to an Experimental Negotiating Agreement providing for the arbitration of unresolved labor contract disputes. But the system did not work, and it was ultimately abandoned, only to be followed by the near-demise of the entire U.S. steel industry.[38]

---

38. *See* Harold S. Roberts, *Roberts' Dictionary of Industrial Relations* 239 (BNA Books 4th ed. 1994).

In other cases, the scope of the arbitration by design has been limited to particular areas, once an actual agreement has been worked out on all other issues. To give but one example, the parties in professional baseball have agreed, but only through the usual collective bargaining arrangements, that individual player compensation can be resolved based on final-offer arbitration. They have refused to move to interest arbitration for their master agreement in negotiating their successive labor contracts, even though repeated breakdowns in collective bargaining have resulted in five strikes and three lockouts since 1972.[39] These breakdowns were in the early years of collective bargaining, when neither side had experience in dealing with the other. Five of the dislocations took place in the decade between 1972 and 1982; two in the decade between 1982 and 1992; one in the decade between 1992 and 2002; and none thereafter. That pattern suggests that we should expect high levels of disruption in the early periods under EFCA because we are in the early stages of the learning curve, where neither side has realistic expectations of how the process will work or what it can expect to derive from it.

The targeted system of final-offer arbitration now in place works because the standard player agreements reduce the disagreement to a single number—the salary—in a contract that lasts for a single year.[40] Each party submits a number and the arbitrator chooses the number that is closest to his own estimate of the player's worth. If the player demands $2 million and the club offers only $1 million, the arbitrator will side with the player if his estimate of the player's one-year worth is over $1.5 million, and with the team if that estimate is under $1.5 million. Under this system, each party knows

    39. The Major League Baseball Players Association reports "[t]here have been five strikes (1972, 1980, 1981, 1985 and 1994–95) and the owners have locked out the players three times (1973, 1976 and 1990)" (http://mlbplayers.mlb.com/pa/info/faq.jsp#1966).

    40. For discussion *see* Spencer R. Gordon, Final Offer Arbitration in the New Era of Major League Baseball, bepress paper 1326, *available at* http://law.bepress.com/cgi/view content.cgi?article=6219&context=expresso.

that it faces an inescapable dilemma. The expected value of its contract will increase as its bid becomes more aggressive (high for the player and low for the team), but that expected value will simultaneously be reduced as aggressive bids always carry with them a lower probability of success. Those two numbers—chance of success and desirability of outcome—are inversely related, so ideally each party would like to pick that figure which is a dollar closer to the anticipated arbitral award than its rival's figure. That process leads to a compression in the bids, so that the gap is usually reduced. The residual uncertainties tend to drive both sides to a settlement, often for long-term negotiated contracts that contain far more complex compensation packages.

There is no possible transference of this system to the world of interest arbitration under EFCA, where the parameters can never be limited to a single variable. At this point, the question is what provisions should be included in an agreement, and how should they be integrated with each other. The traditional form of labor arbitration involved seasoned professionals with close knowledge of the relevant industry and its practices, to which courts have given a great deal of deference.[41] Yet such deference is wholly inappropriate in this context, especially for businesses that were nonunion, where there is no accumulated wisdom to which any arbitrator could turn. A huge demand for arbitrators would test a system that is not geared up to meet it, and the likely source of arbitrators will be the public sector, where the slow pace of innovation and rigid styles of doing business give rise to precisely the wrong mindset.

Where should conscientious arbitrators turn for guidance? There are no obvious comparables among nonunion firms, because their business approaches will differ greatly. So the tendency will be to look to the same unionized firms that have lost market share to their nonunionized rivals, largely because union firms use static paradigms that have long been discarded in nonunion settings. One

41. *See supra* note 1.

obvious issue is job classifications. Union contracts normally do not allow workers in one job category to be pressed into service at a moment's notice to do work that falls outside their job descriptions. But even the casual shopper can observe the length of checkout lines, which are likely to be shorter at nonunion stores, which train all their personnel to operate cash registers to keep the customer traffic flowing.

Any decision to impose union work rules on a nonunion firm, therefore, has profound anticompetitive effects by lowering the best so that the worst can continue to compete. It is as though the labor law were being used to cartelize an industry—and in an inefficient form, at that—in ways that would be improper under the antitrust laws with their focus on the preservation of consumer welfare through the protection of vigorous competition.

Nor would it make sense to compare the nonunion operations at one firm in an industry with those of another. One key advantage of competition is that it allows different businesses to experiment with different business models. Labor arbitration will degenerate into a branch of industrial policy if it is construed to require uniformity on these matters. Interest arbitration will make it difficult for each firm to keep its preferred method of business operations in place no matter what its competitors do. The crippling effects of this system seem evident, which is why so few firms ever agree to it voluntarily. And the situation would be still worse if arbitrators thought that they should confer among themselves before settling on decrees in particular cases. That approach is certainly not required under EFCA, but nothing under the statute prohibits a single panel charged with many cases from taking just this approach.

In sum, the difficulties with compulsory interest arbitration are so manifest that Congress should reject it forthwith.

CHAPTER 3

THE SOCIAL CONSEQUENCES OF UNIONIZATION

AN INTEREST GROUP ANALYSIS

The social consequences of the Employee Free Choice Act need examination because there is much evidence that employment laws are perceived as the number one regulatory threat facing American firms today—even without EFCA.[1] The adoption of EFCA will only compound the problem with its twin threats of card check and compulsory arbitration. As a theoretical matter, legal reforms can never produce social gains by shrinking the size of the pie, which is what always happens when administrative costs go up and productive output goes down. In this chapter, I predict how EFCA will affect four groups: unions, employees, employers, and all third parties.

The analysis of the first point does not require any subtlety. Union dues fuel union activities. Each provision of EFCA adds fuel to the fire by increasing the ability of unions to organize and to undertake political activities that protect or enhance their economic clout inside the workplace. Unions have to be chalked up as unambiguous winners from EFCA. The other three groups require some more consideration. The bottom line is that workers find themselves, at best, in an ambiguous position, which explains their

---

1. Amy Miller, Corporate Counsel, August 18, 2008. For the related survey data, *see* http://www.law.com/jsp/article.jsp?id = 1202423810256.

divided loyalties. From the outset they must be able to secure from unionization advantages that offset the loss of the secret ballot and the opportunity to ratify or reject any final settlement—both now exclusive union prerogatives. Employers are unambiguous losers, which explains their opposition. The public at large also loses, but the consequences of the legislation are sufficiently indirect that the public's views on the question may not track the probable economic consequences of the legislation.

THE AMBIGUOUS UNION MEMBER INTEREST: A LARGER SHARE OF A SMALLER PIE

The easiest way to understand the ambiguities of the employees' position is to ask what they can gain or lose from engaging in union activity. The traditional position, acknowledged even by union supporters, is that the NLRA allows unions to exercise on behalf of their members some degree of monopoly power, which in turn allows them to raise wages, reduce hours, and otherwise improve working conditions. In writing about this topic 25 years ago, economists Richard Freeman and James Medoff noted:

> Most, if not all, unions have monopoly power, which they can use to raise wages above competitive levels. Assuming that the competitive system works perfectly, these wage increases have harmful economic effects, reducing the national output and distorting the distribution of income. The analysis of unions as monopolies focuses on the magnitude of the union markup of wages and traces the ways in which this markup causes firms to lower employment and output, thereby harming economic efficiency and altering the distribution of income.[2]

In one sense, their candid admission attributes to unions more influence over wages than they now exert. The economy today is

_____

2. Richard B. Freeman & James L. Medoff, *What Do Unions Do?* 6 (1984).

more competitive than it was twenty five years ago when Freeman and Medoff were writing. The increased pace of global trade and improved systems of transportation and communication expand the market, which in turn makes it more difficult for niche unions to acquire and maintain monopoly power—which is one reason why unions oppose free trade agreements. Union monopoly power is a constant threat but not a uniform presence. That monopoly power, however, can be increased through legislation. Some historical data point to a substantial increment in wages that union members have over nonunion members. University of California-Berkeley Professor Harley Shaiken notes "Bureau of Labor Statistics data that indicate a union wage advantage of 28.1 percent for wages and 43.7 percent of total compensation—wages and benefits."[3] To be sure, these differentials look large. It is therefore necessary to correct the numbers by controlling for other features of the two cohorts of workers. Shaiken concludes—and I cannot vouch for his numbers—that the wage premium for union workers is 14.7 percent across all groups.[4] Still more impressive numbers are bandied about—again without documentation—by Anna Burger of SEIU, who claims, "Workers in unions earn 30 percent higher wages, are 59 percent more likely to have employer-based health coverage, and four times more likely to have pension benefits."[5] But again she offers no articulation of the underlying assumptions. Independent economic estimates of the wage increment attributable to union power are less striking, and vary between 8 percent and 20 percent, with a median of around 15 percent.[6]

    3. *Strengthening America's Middle Class Through the Employee Free Choice Act: Hearing on H.R. 800 before the H. Subcomm. Health, Employment, Labor, and Pensions,* 110th Cong. 4 (2007) (statement of Harley Shaiken, Professor, UC Berkeley) *available at* http://www.aflcio.org/joinaunion/voiceatwork/efca/upload/EFCA_Shaiken_2007 0208.pdf.

    4. *Id.*

    5. Mike Link, Anna Burger: The Economic Recovery Program Our Nation Needs, SEIU Blog, December 12, 2008, at http://www.seiu.org/2008/12/anna-burger-the-economic-recovery-program-our-nation-needs.php.

    6. *See,* David Blanchflower, *The Role and Influence of Trade Unions in the OECD,* 22 (London School of Economics, Center for Economic Performance Discussion Paper no. 310, 1996); David Blanchflower, *Changes over Time in Union Relative Wage Effects in Great*

The identification of this wage and benefit premium, however calculated, does not offer any measure of overall social welfare, but only gives some crude measure of the level of supracompetitive profits that unions can obtain within this system. Nor does it give any indication of how these gains are, or should be, distributed among the workers who received them. As Freeman and Medoff recognize, the overall situation is far more complex because unions do not operate like business entities. In general, business entities are able to suppress conflicts of interest among shareholders by structuring their holdings so that they share pro rata by size of stakes in firms' gains and losses.[7] It is precisely to preserve these parallel interests that publicly traded corporations usually have only a single class of common stock. The individual interests of union members, however, often diverge from one another. Seniority matters among the rank and file, and its rigorous protection in union contracts is no testimony to its efficiency, as Freeman and Medoff suggest,[8] for there is little evidence that it is adopted in nonunion firms. Rather, the strict adherence to seniority systems reflects the additional political clout that senior workers have, given that the governance structure favors their interests when it comes to layoffs.[9] In addition, unions have to speak for their retired members, especially on pension and health care issues, and make provision for the hiring of new members. Political power within the union is positively correlated with longevity of union membership, which increases the potential of intergenerational conflicts.

Britain and the United States, 4 (NBER Technical Report Working Paper No. 6100, 1997) (15 percent); Randel Filer et al., *The Economics of Work and Pay* (Harper Collins 6th ed. 1996) 8 percent to 12 percent); Bernt Bratsberg and James Ragan, Changes in the Union Wage Premium by Industry, 56, 80 Indus. & Lab. Rel. Rev. 65 (2002) (22 percent in the 1970s).

7. Freeman & Medoff supra note 2, at 6.

8. *Id.* at 15.

9. A compromise position on promotions and layoffs often favors seniority unless the firm can demonstrate the superior qualifications of a junior worker. *See, e.g.*, the specimen agreements in *Steelworkers* and *Warrior Gulf* supra note 11 (Chapter 2).

Some matters affect all workers equally while others trigger conflicts of interest. Laying bare these common conflicts helps explain
why workers are of two minds over union membership. On one
side, there are many union enthusiasts for whom solidarity is a
watchword. But this group is not a random sample of the overall
population. Workers whose views differ will tend to gravitate away
from strong union firms and from industries with strong union
presence. There is no reason to think that the level of union support
in existing units translates to equal levels of support in the general
population. Quite the contrary, there are many costs associated
with union membership that explain the reluctance of nonunionized workers to cast their lot with unions.

First, union membership does not come cheap. In 2000, it was
reported that union dues eat up on average 1.25 percent of the
paycheck,[10] a figure that seems stable.[11] Union activities can eat up
a fraction more. Some portions of the increase in gross pay are thus
offset by the increase in union-related expenses. These costs are
compounded by the need for workers to spend time on union
affairs, be it to run committees or vote in elections, or cooperate
with or oppose the union on particular questions. Union democracy does not come free, and operates fitfully at best. The refusal of
workers to participate in their collective affairs is costly. Standing
aside in union elections, for example, could result in the selection
of union officers who are antagonistic to some of the absentees'
interests. Not participating in union governance could lead to a
weakening of union institutions or isolation from fellow union
members. It is harder for workers to navigate a system with dual
union and management governance than it is for them to deal with
a single employer.

Second, unionization dulls long-term worker prospects for

---

10. John W. Budd & In-Gang Na, The Union Membership Wage Premium for Employees Covered by Collective Bargaining Agreements, 18 J. Labor Econ.783, 803 (2000).

11. *See* Mark Brenner, Give your Union a Dues Checkup, Labor Notes, *available at*
http://www.labornotes.org/node/908.

advancement—a consequence that will affect younger workers more than older ones, and able workers more than mediocre ones. The complex dual governance structure in which both management and labor play a part can have major implications for employees. Low-level workers find it easier to gain access to management positions in nonunion settings. The Supreme Court has long upheld the NLRB regulations that exclude from statutory coverage any employees with access to confidential files and information related to management functions.[12] The theory is that dual loyalties are not acceptable for sensitive positions. But this narrow interpretive rule could not reach all cases of dual loyalty unless it completely gutted the NLRA's basic collective bargaining mandate. All union members, no matter what their station, have dual loyalties, which may make some management representatives reluctant to share with union members that type of information that could be used against them later. The lines between union and nonunion workers can harden so that it is risky for managers to mentor union workers with an eye to promotion.[13] A nonunionized firm is much less worried about dual loyalties, and thus is able to give rank-and-file workers more of the sensitive information that can help them learn about the business as a spur to personal advancement. In a similar vein, no unionized employer may offer additional benefits to workers of exceptional diligence or skill unless authorized by the collective bargaining agreement. These constraints limit the upward mobility of workers within the firm, by creating a wall of separation between union workers and management.

---

12. *See* NLRB v. Hendricks Cty. Rural Elec. Membership Corp., 454 U.S. 170 (1981).

13. The Re-Empowerment of Skilled and Professional Employees and Construction Tradesworkers (RESPECT) Act (H.R. 1644, 110th Cong., 1st Sess. (2007)) is a legislative initiative that would operate to increase the dual loyalties between supervisors and rank-and-file employees, by narrowing the NLRA's definition of "supervisor," effectively converting many supervisors into rank-and-file employees. At this point we could replicate the situation that exists, for example, in the New York City public schools in which teachers are members of one union, and principals and other supervisors are members of a second. The increased union cooperation cuts against the separation of management from labor.

The wall can get quite high. In many settings it is a ULP for an employer to alter working arrangements or resolve grievances with individual workers without going through the union. As the grievance process becomes more formal, the Supreme Court has held that no individual worker has the right to control his own case, even though section 9(a) of the NLRA appears to authorize that result.[14] Today the grievance can only go forward if the union decides to press it, except in the few cases where the union is found to have acted in bad faith.[15] This interposed layer of control makes it difficult for workers to calculate their net advantage from union membership. Accordingly, many workers, especially stronger workers, may sensibly conclude that the short-term wage increases from unionization are substantially offset by the reduction in their long-term prospects of advancement.

Third, many union defenders take pride in the increased equalization of wages that unions introduce into the workplace. But this parity is a double-edged sword given its adverse impact on firm efficiency. As a matter of economic theory, an efficient firm will set pay to reflect the (marginal) contribution that each worker makes to the firm. Cost-justified wage differentials will be common as firms have little desire to engage in cross-subsidies among members of its workforce. Pay some workers too little relative to their contribution and they will leave; pay them too much and you will lose out financially to the competition. But unions cannot work by this simple metric because of their need to share the wealth among all

---

14. NLRA § 9a. (5 U.S.C. § 159a), ". . . any individual employee or a group of employees shall have the right at any time to present grievances to their employer and to have such grievances adjusted, without the intervention of the bargaining representative, as long as the adjustment is not inconsistent with the terms of a collective-bargaining contract or agreement then in effect. . . ."

15. *See* Vaca v. Sipes, 386 U.S. 171 (1967). *Vaca* relied heavily on Archibald Cox, *Rights under a Labor Agreement*, 69 HARV. L. REV. 601 (1956), which thought that the need for collective control applied with equal force to contract negotiation and grievance arbitration. For a defense of the worker's right to press his own grievance, see my student note, Richard A. Epstein Individual Control of Grievances under Vaca v. Sipes, 77 Yale L. J. 559, 563–64, 577–78 (1968).

union members in order to maintain their majority coalition. In response to these governance pressures, the union will tend to narrow wage differences among workers in different classifications in order to hold the bargaining unit together. Skilled workers, if outnumbered in the bargaining unit, could easily oppose unionization on just this ground.

The concern is long-standing. As early as the 1960s, the UAW had to enter into special agreements to resolve the long-standing grievances of its skilled workers.[16] The problem occurs today. Here is one example in hospitals. Let all nurses be put into the same unit and wages will level off, which will tend to create shortages on hard beats like oncology and intensive care, and surpluses in pediatrics and obstetrics, where happy occasions outnumber sad ones. Similar conflicts arise when unions have to reconcile seniority lists when two units merge.[17] The firm's inability to maintain wage differentials could compromise the firm's competitive standing, leading to across-the-board reductions in wages and work force.

These problems are compounded because technical innovation and global competition require quick adoption of new business models. These shifts are hard to negotiate in advance, even when both sides are committed to the collective bargaining process. Rigid union job categories impede renegotiation of the collective bargaining agreement. Risk-averse workers will tend to favor the status quo. And that bias will be strengthened by the heavy transaction costs of renegotiating a deal that leaves each union group happy. Ordinary firms in private markets typically respond to adverse economic circumstances by firing some workers.[18] More recently, there has been a move toward unpaid furloughs and extended closings as

16. *See* N.Y. Times, October 20, 1967, at 1, discussed in Epstein *supra* note 15, at 562, n. 14.

17. *See* Humphrey v. Moore, 375 U.S. 335 (1964), finding that the duty of fair representation did not protect the dissident workers when the union integrated seniority lists on length of service.

18. *See* Truman F. Bewley, *Why Wages Don't Fall During a Recession* (Harvard University Press 1999).

part of a general effort to keep the workforce intact for an eventual economic turnaround.[19] Their judgment is that it is too costly to maintain a large workforce of part-time employees who are likely to be both resentful and underemployed. Morale and output will both suffer. Severance, often with some economic package, is the preferred alternative in most firms. That strategy will not be as attractive to unions for whom the dismissal of any worker means a loss of union membership and a corresponding loss of dues income. So there are efforts to provide various forms of compensation to individual workers, such as the automobile workers who continue to draw paychecks as union members so long as they are "available" for work in some facility.[20] The upshot is that the unionized firm could easily lag behind its more nimble rivals.

Some unions understand this risk and encourage various kinds of training programs to earn worker support. Shaiken in his congressional testimony quotes James Kaster, president of UAW 1715, representing the famed General Motors plant in Lordstown, Ohio: "If we don't make a profit, we don't have a plant."[21] All too true, but not quite in the sense he intended. General Motors is on the ropes; total union membership at the company is down sharply.[22] Lordstown does relatively well because it makes small cars. But there is an ongoing union battle over "flow rights" to Lordstown

---

19. "A growing number of employers, hoping to avoid or limit layoffs, are introducing four-day workweeks, unpaid vacations and voluntary or enforced furloughs, along with wage freezes, pension cuts and flexible work schedules. These employers are still cutting labor costs, but hanging onto the labor." Matt Richel, More Companies Cut Labor Costs Without Layoffs, N.Y. Times, Dec. 22, 2008, at A1. The article notes, however, that layoffs are still the most common form of dealing with cutbacks, which is reflected in the increase in unemployment levels toward the end of 2008.

20. Jeffrey McCracken, Money for Nothing: U.S. Car Companies Pay Hundreds of Millions of Dollars in Wages to Idled Workers, Wall. St. J. Classroom Ed., May 2006 *available at* http://wsjclassroom.com/archive/06may/auto2_jobsbank.htm.

21. Shaiken, *supra* note 3, at 6.

22. In 1984, GM employed 350,000 UAW workers while as of the end of 2006 only 89,000 GM employees were represented by unions. Peter Perl, Settlement or Possible Strike; Auto Workers Target General Motors, Wash. Post, Sept. 7, 1984, at A2. General Motors Corp., Annual Report (Form 10-K), at 18 (Mar. 14, 2007).

from the shuttered GM plant in Moraine.[23] The truth is that plant closings have been routine at GM, even before its implosion at the end of 2008. Clearly someone has miscalculated the amount of "free cash" available in collective bargaining negotiations at Moraine and elsewhere. It is no accident that the former Big Three automobile companies have been in dire distress for sometime. It is not that onerous union contracts are the sole source of their unease: the protected dealership networks must bear some share of the blame. But by the same token the huge capital infusions at GM and Chrysler have proved unavailing. What is most instructive is the likely outcomes of the deals orchestrated in the White House, which makes the government the owner of 50 percent of the stock of General Motors, and the UAW pension a majority owner, with a 55 percent stake, in Chrysler.[24] In both cases, the senior debentures holders have received far less favorable deals through the political processes than they would have received in bankruptcy. These ongoing negotiations could still fall apart, but no matter which way they are resolved the legacy costs of the strong union movement put the Big Three, or what is left of them, at a marked disadvantage

---

23. *See* Thomas Gnau, IUE-CWA voices irritation at delay of GM contract talks. "The union seeks rights for members to transfer to other GM plants, including Lordstown after Moraine site closes." Dayton B2B, August 14, 2008, *available at* http://www.daytondaily news.com/n/content/oh/story/business/2008/08/13/ddn081308gmupdateweb.html?cxtype = rss&cxsvc = 7&cxcat = 59. On the closing of the GM plants in Moraine, and Janesville Wisconsin, and the Chrysler plant in Newark, Delaware—all of which produced SUVs, *see* Nick Bunkley & Bill Vlasic, *It's the End of the Line for S.U.V.'s*, N.Y. Times, Dec. 24, 2008, at B1. For another account of the bloodletting from the World Socialist Web Site, *see* Jerry Isaacs & Colin Davis, New union contracts clear way for US automakers to cut 50,000 jobs *available at* http://www.wsws.org/articles/2003/oct2003/uaw-o01.shtml October 1, 2003.

24. For one recent account see Chrysler bankrupt, GM hurting, Chattanooga Times Free Press, May 2, 2009, http://timesfreepress.com/news/2009/may/02/chrysler-bankrupt-gm-hurting/?opinionfreepress. In assessing the wreckage, the story notes that both companies have been able to improve the quality of their cars in recent years after some lackluster management, and continues: "Probably the biggest was their expensive, complicated contracts with employees represented by the United Auto Workers union. Those contracts boosted the cost of their cars by perhaps $1,800 or more, with no additional value to car buyers, even as foreign car companies were building cars in U.S. factories under more sustainable conditions.

relative to foreign corporations that do not have to bear these multiple burdens.

One of the knottiest problems in union negotiations involves the implicit conflict between the senior workers, who need the business to last only long enough to secure their high wages and retirement benefits, and the junior workers who necessarily have a longer time horizon. That conflict is one of degree, not in kind. But the difference in preferences can be large enough that the dominant senior faction will push hard to reap its short-term benefits while leaving retirees and younger members in the lurch. These pension arrangements could be destabilized under EFCA. Pension and other retirement benefits are mandatory terms, so that an arbitration agreement could reduce the pensions of some workers and increase those of others, given that no prior contractual understandings are protected against revision under the *J.I. Case* rule that allows collective bargaining agreements to abrogate otherwise valid labor contracts.[25] Even conflict of interest is not as stark as that explicitly acknowledged whenever unions negotiate two-tier wage packages, whereby *future* employees receive far less in their compensation packages than current workers. It's no surprise that the UAW negotiated just this type of deal in order to gain $1 billion in new work. Here is the indictment of that deal on the World Socialist Web Site:

> The UAW also jettisoned the principle of "equal pay for equal work" by agreeing to lower wages for new hires at Delphi and Visteon (the parts company spun off from Ford), which currently employ 30,000 UAW workers. The companies are seeking to establish a permanent two-tier wage system, in which new hires work for vastly lower starting wages and benefits—in line with other suppliers—and can never catch up to workers who were hired before the current contract.
>
> The UAW and the two parts suppliers will meet within 90 days of the contract ratification to work out the extent of the wage and

25. J.I. Case. Co. v. NLRB, 321 U.S. 332 (1944), discussed *supra* note 1 (Chapter 1).

benefit cuts. Delphi and Visteon workers will have no vote on the matter.

As one worker noted, the two-tier wages will further break up the solidarity of auto workers. In future contracts, the companies are sure to tell newer workers the only way they can pay for wage improvements is to vote for pension reductions for the company's tens of thousands of retirees.[26]

Why be surprised? The union has preserved the monopoly profits for its dominant faction while acceding to a competitive wage for the new arrivals who had no voice in the bargaining unit when the agreement was negotiated. No wonder one worker said, "The UAW is no longer a union. They are all sellouts. They are just looking out for their own interests."[27] Too harsh, perhaps, because desperate situations require extreme actions.

The debacle in the automobile industry has not spread to all industries. Some unions do better than others, within and across industries. The histories of these relationships are filled with twists and turns, so that it is impossible for anyone to summarize accurately the path of any particular negotiation. It is critical to understand why this wide variation in management-union relations is virtually inevitable given the uncertain operation of union democracy under current law. The outcomes of union elections and card checks are often determined by a few votes one way or the other. It takes very little to displace a cooperative union president with a firebrand who wants to take high risks to secure high returns for workers—or the reverse. The contrast between the relative labor peace at Southwest Airlines and the constant tumult at Northwest Airlines show how much one union can diverge from another.[28]

26. Isaacs & Davis supra note 32 (Chapter 1).

27. *Id.*

28. The National Mediation Board reports that under the Railway Labor act since 1998 Northwestern workers have gone on two strikes for a total of 431 days while there have been no strikes at Southwest. National Mediation Board, *Strike Report: U.S. Airlines Under the Railway Labor Act, available at* http://www.nmb.gov/publicinfo/airline-strikes.html.

Union membership creates another form of instability that workers could rationally wish to avoid: the statutory framework for collective bargaining negotiations, which impose on both sides the obligation to bargain in good faith. By conscious design this results in a bilateral monopoly situation in which there is no unique wage level for any given output as there is in a competitive market.[29] The union, as exclusive representative of the workers, must bargain with management. Management must bargain with this union. Neither side has alternatives. There is no way that the management can just refuse to deal or seek out new trading partners as in competitive markets.

This structure matters. As a matter of economic theory, there is a huge level of indeterminacy about the terms and conditions of these contracts, and much dispute over wages. In many negotiations, there is a large bargaining range: the minimum that the union will accept is less than the maximum that the firm will offer. (On salary, for example, if the union might accept $20 per hour, and the management may be prepared to offer up to $30, the bargaining range is $10. In this simple example, there is no unique range, as much depends on the bargaining strategies of the two sides.) Markets with bilateral monopolies are always more difficult to operate than competitive ones where the gap between the offering and asking price quickly disappears. Accordingly, the good faith negotiations are far more artificial, scripted, and complex than those that exist in a nonunion environment where take-it-or-leave-it offers can be made on either side at far lower cost. Negotiations in competitive markets rarely have catastrophic consequences when thcy break down, because both sides can go elsewhere. Not so when collective bargaining negotiations break down under the NLRA. Strikes and lockouts can arise, with disruptions in production or service. In the long run, few firms, new or established, will choose to invest capital in environments where such investments can be

---

29. NLRA § 8 (5 U.S.C. § 158).

held hostage to union demands. Some firms will contract or go out of business. Other firms will invest their capital in the nonunion portions of the business in order to realize a more stable set of returns.

These consequences are neither obscure nor improbable. Workers who sense the downward spiral of union relationships could easily prefer the long-term stability of nonunion relationships to the high risk/high return strategy from unionization. The auto workers, steel workers, and rubber workers unions are vivid illustrations of how risky union membership can turn out to be. The lesson will not be lost on some workers who will shy away from new businesses that are saddled with union representation. The defenders of EFCA studiously ignore these issues, even though a clear awareness of these industrial casualties is critical for any worker to make an intelligent choice. Employer speech and the frank expression of opinion—both protected under federal law[30]— can often be of great service to the firm's workers as they debate among themselves the pros and cons of union representation.

The Employer's Interest under Collective Bargaining: A Smaller Share of a Smaller Pie

The ambiguity in worker attitudes and preferences stems from the fact that possible monopoly wages could offset the overall productivity losses of the firm. Different workers will make different assessments on this fundamental trade-off, so that views can run the gamut from deep devotion to fierce opposition to labor unions. The employer interest does not suffer from any such ambiguity. The firm gets the smaller share of the smaller pie, and thus loses both ways from unionization. It is no wonder that many successful

---

30. NLRA § 8(c), 29 U.S.C. § 158(c).

firms are so openly adamant about resisting unions.[31] They do not have to calculate the precise magnitude of the losses to know that unions create the double whammy. Their only question is how best to respond to the risk.

The defenders of unionization in general, and of EFCA in particular, write as if employer resistance to unionization were an inexplicable and lamentable feature of the business landscape. They do not seem to believe that the opposition to unions is either rational or defensible. In order to make that case respectable, they put forward a "second face" of unionization which they claim generates sufficient social gains to make the entire collective bargaining enterprise worth protecting by statute. Freeman and Medoff exemplify this approach when they point to "The Collective Voice/Institutional Response Face" of unionization as the source of the putative efficiency gains to offset the monopoly wages that unions sometimes extract from the firm.

A heavy burden of proof lies on those who think that this "second face" of unionization sweeps aside all employer opposition. If unions could provide firms benefits that these firms could not generate for themselves, key executives would be jumping over chairs to embrace the first union to knock on the door. After all, why would these profit-making soulless entities resist unions if they held the only keys to improved labor performance? In this topsy-turvy world, a nonunionized firm should fret if its rival obtained a competitive advantage from being unionized! And it should announce its willingness to accept unionization in order to restore its competitive position. It never happens; in all cases, the story line runs in the opposite direction. It is far more likely that a firm will accede

---

31. *See, e.g.,* Wal-Mart formerly stating on its corporate Web site, "At Wal-Mart, we respect the individual rights of our associates and encourage them to express their ideas, comments, and concerns. Because we believe in maintaining an environment of open communication, we do not believe there is a need for third party representation." Available at http://www.pbs.org/wgbh/pages/frontline/shows/walmart/transform/e mployment.html. There is little question in my mind that the silent resentments of management run more deeply than their public statements.

reluctantly to unionization only if the union can credibly promise that its rivals will labor under the same (dis)advantage in order to minimize the expected losses.[32]

The "second face" claim boils down to an argument of "false consciousness." Virtually all employers in the United States are presumed ignorant of their own business interests when they oppose unions whose innovations could enhance productivity and profits. Not possible: these managers have worked too hard, and have too much on-the-ground knowledge, to be dismissed as uninformed cranks or ideological zealots standing in the path of progress. Their consistent and intense resistance to unionization should be regarded as well-nigh conclusive evidence of their deep conviction that unionization leads to net losses for the firm. They have every incentive to be right. The labor sympathizers in economics and law have every incentive to be wrong.

What then could lead learned economists to embrace the opposite conclusion? One argument urged by Freeman and Medoff is that collective bargaining is needed to overcome a "public goods problem" associated with firm production.[33] Their list of these so-called public goods is impressive: "Safety conditions, lighting, heating, the speed of the production line, the firm's formal grievance procedure, pension plan, and policies on matters such as layoffs, work-sharing, cyclical wage adjustments, and promotion."[34] They conclude that a competitive market will fail to grapple with these collective issues, all on the implicit assumption that the only private good that firms supply their workers is the money in their paychecks. Otherwise the firm will be plagued by "free rider" problems among workers that a union backed by a union security provision is able to overcome.

---

32. *See, e.g.*, Duplex Printing Press Co. v. Deering, 254 U.S. 443, 479–480 (1921), where some firms announced that they would throw off their union contracts unless their competitors acceded to union contracts. For discussion, *see* Richard A. Epstein, *How Progressives Rewrote the Constitution*, 87–88 (Cato Institute 2006).

33. Freeman & Medoff *supra* note 2, at 8.

34. Freeman & Medoff *supra* note 2, at 8–9.

My initial response to this broad definition of public goods is one of wonderment. If these so-called public goods problems were acute, how could any of the thousands of nonunion firms ever be as efficient as their union rivals? Indeed, how could they function at all? And yet somehow, before the arrival of the union, they seem to solve these issues of employment relations by institutional, contractual, and social means. Why? Because there is no public goods problem at all. The classic public goods problem arises when *no* individual has the power to exclude, so that the private investments by each are less than they would be if all could coordinate their behavior.[35] The standard illustration involves the street lamps on the public road abutting fifty homes. The lamps shed light equally on all in amounts equally desired by all. If parties had to rely on individual voluntary actions to fund the street lights, each individual would sit tight because he or she knows that he receives only a fraction of the gain—2 percent—that the improvements generate for all. Consider a common case where the total social gain from installing street lights is one hundred and twenty-five, and the total social cost of installation is fifty. Acting alone, no self-interested person would invest fifty from which he derived only two and a half units of private gain, the same as everyone else. But what if we could get all the individuals to cooperate by contract under which each agrees to contribute the one unit needed to fund the venture from which each would derive one and a half in gain? The voluntary approach typically won't work because of the high transaction costs of coordinating the activities of fifty individuals, each of whom has an incentive to hold out. This example offers a clear instance of market failure because some individuals will hold out on the assumption that they would rather have lights funded by others than pay anything themselves. Since the costs of coordinating fifty persons—some cooperative, some not—are likely to exceed

---

35. *See* for the classic account, Mancur Olson, *The Logic of Collective Action* (Harvard University Press 1965).

the potential one hundred units of gain, a solution that everyone wants is one that no one can achieve. Coercion in the form of a special assessment leaves everyone better off than before, given the identity of their positions.

This coordination problem, however, disappears if the lights are needed as part of a planned unit development. The project owner puts in the lights at the appropriate cost and then reaps some additional value from the sale of the individual units, the price of which is raised to reflect the PUD services tied to the unit. The transaction costs for the improvements are no greater than for those of the individual units. That one institutional adjustment eliminates the free rider and collective action problems that called for a system of special assessments. And it does so in a way that allows for a more accurate judgment on what improvements are needed and a fairer allocation of costs, given that all potential buyers can value the entire package before making their decisions. Even those workers who do not value the common improvements at their allocated costs need not stay away. If the gains from the purchase of the individual unit exceed the losses from some (or even all) of the common improvements, it may still make sense to join in. Yet knowing the situation in advance is likely to reduce the variance of group members, which makes it easier to handle the collective action problems that will inevitably arise in the governance of the PUD.

These arguments carry over to the workplace without a hitch. Now the employer stands in the position of the project developer and the workers as potential unit owners. The employer knows that employees have diverse interests and he seeks to design wage and benefit packages that meet their individual demands. There is no need to rely on collective union mechanisms to supply common goods to workers from heterogeneous backgrounds. The public goods analysis is irrelevant in the context of a firm workplace because the firm coordinates its activities for the benefit of all. No worker will enter into a deal that leaves him or her worse off than before, taking into account both the private benefits of wages and the firm-specific public goods relating to working conditions and the like. The firm is, of course, well aware of the inevitable spillovers among workers, and will therefore set wages and terms in ways that take into account both the direct and indirect consequences of a decision.

To see why, take certain elements that must be supplied to all workers in a unit if they are supplied to any: lighting is such an example. Here the firm has a solid feedback mechanism. If it considers a lighting pattern that one group of workers values at plus ten and another group values at minus forty, it will reject the alternative because it will have to compensate workers for their net change in position of minus thirty. At this point it thinks of another form of lighting, or it decides that physical separation into two groups makes sense for these workers. If separation is not feasible, then the firm may reconfigure its workforce so that its members have greater homogeneity with respect to these firm-specific common goods. The same is true with such issues as injuries on the job, where the wages offered by the firm must offset the potential losses to the worker, leading once again to the internalization of both costs and benefits. The firm will therefore worry about the level of safety, lest it be forced to pay excessive wages.[36]

The fundamental point that Freeman and Medoff miss is that the ability of the firm to internalize these choices incentivizes it toward an efficient solution without union intervention. There is no coordination problem similar to that with public lighting. This result, moreover, applies not just to employment, but works with equal power for such diverse organizations as corporations, partnerships, and condominium associations. Make one person or group the hub around which all other individuals work, and the public goods problem disappears. At this point the employer is in a position to integrate resources. *None* of the particular features of

---

36. *See*, on this point, W. Kip Viscusi, *Risk by Choice* (Harvard University Press 1983).

the employment contract that Freeman and Medoff mention count as public goods. The union is at best the fifth wheel on the coach. In most cases it is far worse, because the divided control that it introduces over these issues impedes the ability of the employer to make the appropriate tradeoffs across all persons who are in the firm and who work with it. The union goal to maximize the profits of its members is inconsistent with the employer's goal to maximize the value of the firm, which includes shareholder and nonunion employee interests as well. The only serious matter to debate is the level of inefficiency that these split power arrangements introduce. There are no social gains from the internal strife and high transaction costs introduced by a regime of divided control.

Equally dubious is the next rationale that Freeman and Medoff invoke to defend unionization on social welfare grounds: "A second reason why collective action is necessary is that workers who are tied to a firm are unlikely to reveal their true preferences to an employer for fear that an employer would fire them." The same theme is echoed in Shaiken's testimony, relying on Freeman and Medoff: "Without unions, day-to-day competitive pressures leave workers with quitting as the only option to address serious problems, a costly solution for all concerned."[37] What?!? The truth is precisely the opposite. Precisely because quitting is a costly solution, competitive pressures on nonunionized firms will lead them to adopt, post-haste, less drastic solutions. Employers have a strong interest in forestalling senseless levels of turnover and costly training of replacement workers with a similarly short tenure.

The description of behavior in nonunion firms defies common experience. There are thousands of interactions each day, formal and informal, in which employee preferences are revealed, openly and enthusiastically—and for good reason. The suggestion box is not a union invention. Employee bonuses for useful improvements in manufacturing and marketing do not violate some unwritten

---

37. Shaiken *supra* note 3, at 6.

employer code. Successful managers are fond of saying that their people are their most important asset. They make strenuous efforts to hire, retain, and promote able workers. No firm has ever grown by firing more workers than it hires. Yet the words "recruitment" and "retention" never once enter into the lexicon of union supporters. Nevertheless, references to these problems in tight markets are legion. Here is one quotation drawn almost at random: "It is incredibly difficult to recruit and retain great people," said Judith Itkin, partner in charge of lawyer resources at Hunton & Williams.[38] The article quotes Carol Evans, chief executive officer of Working Mother Media: "Today, with nearly half of law school graduates women, law firms will have to make a fundamental shift in their policies regarding partnership in order to remain competitive. We hope that by recognizing the pioneering firms that have already moved the needle, a paradigm shift will follow." The message has already been heard.

Yes, competition matters, and it flourishes without unions, which impose a barrier between workers and management that impairs the very communications that Freeman and Medoff wish to encourage. I have heard more than one employer lament quietly that he or she could not consult workers directly about various renovations to their workplaces, given that these communications count as unfair labor practices, owing to the union's status as the exclusive bargaining representative of the worker. Rather than try to organize a complex three-ring circus where each interaction may open up the firm to liability under the current contract, the preferred strategy is to fly blind, which closes down lines of communication that good human resource specialists are hired to keep open. Salary is one component of an attractive compensation package, but only one. Everything counts. No informed management team supports a culture of fear and intimidation. The buzzwords are fit,

---

38. Peter Page, Just What Makes a Firm Friendly for Women and Working Mothers?, Nat'l, L. J., Aug. 14, 2008.

a sense of shared mission, openness, and collaboration, as management gurus repeatedly stress.[39]

In this competitive environment, the last thing that an employer wants is an employee who is reticent about his or her criticisms, insights, or demands. Suppose that an employer can supply either benefit package A or B to the worker in the form of benefits at equal cost to itself. Why would it not want to learn which individuals or groups prefer package A to B, when it can make everyone happy by honoring these preferences at no cost? That is why employers commonly offer workers menus of choices involving such matters as pensions, vacations, health insurance, housing allowances, and the like. The firm commits itself to a set of options over which it is indifferent, and then allows each worker separately to pick that bundle of goods that maximizes his or her welfare. That cannot be done without the active solicitation of information, which will only be supplied if workers are confident that it will be used as a basis for future firm action. Workers may receive some compensation for the suggestions made. But even if they do not, it is critical that they not think that everything they say is given the "file and forget" treatment.

Where then lies the claim for union superiority? One common claim is that productivity gains come from reduced employee turn-over in unionized plants, which is said to lead to lower training costs and higher productivity.[40] Again, turnover costs could hardly escape management's attention in a nonunionized plant, given the employer's cost of recruiting replacements. The critical question is

---

39. *See, e.g.,* Jim Collins, *Good to Great: Why Some Companies Make the Leap and Others Don't* 41 (Collins Business 2001) stressing the importance of assembling the right business team with good communication up and down the ranks. "The executives who ignited the transformations from good to great did not first figure out where to drive the bus and then get people to take it there. No, they *first* got the right people on the bus (and the wrong people off the bus), and *then* figured out where to drive it." The point here is that with the right people on the bus it is easier to change directions and to motivate people. These principles apply up and down the work place. The strategies that motivate senior management can be adapted to deal with all sorts of workers in large and small firms alike.

40. *Id.* relying on Freeman & Medoff *supra* note 2, at 94–110.

how to interpret the turnover figures. Freeman and Medoff claim that the turnover rate is low because unions give workers a larger voice within the business, and therefore assume that the monopoly wages they receive, if any, have less to do with their decision to stay. There is no reason, however, to think that one reason is more important than the other. It could easily be the case in some situations that workers hold on to jobs they hate solely because of the monopoly wage. Surely the workers who came day after day to job bank facilities in the automotive industry were doing it only for the money. Yet it was only the need for bailout funds that put these programs to an end.[41]

Stepping back from the particulars, however, the real question about length of job tenure does not concern workers' motives. Rather, it must address any supposed correlation between length of service and the qualifications and willingness of individual workers to contribute to firm productivity. There is no reason to believe that this correlation is uniformly positive. The key question that any firm has to address is which employees should be retained and which ones should be let go. These decisions are frequently distorted at both ends by union agreements. New workers are often subject to short probationary periods, after which their rights are fully protected under the collective bargaining agreement. These provisions often force management to terminate workers prematurely because of the fear that they will not work out once they become permanent employees. In unregulated firms, workers on the bubble could be extended for an additional period during which they could hone their skills and improve their performance. There is little gain to blocking the orderly development of human capital. But in a union context, getting a union waiver on the probation question raises large institutional issues. Grant it once and it could be requested a second and a third time, until the original agreement

---

41. The Chrysler job banks program was terminated in January 2009 in order to allow the company to qualify for Congressional bailout funds. http://www.autoblog.com/2009/01/25/chrysler-job-bank-going-on-hiatus-monday/.

is shot through with holes. So the safe course is one of initial intransigence. Keep strictly to the program lest the entire edifice crumble.

The rigidity of collective bargaining agreements also creates immense difficulties at the opposite end of the work cycle. In many public and private settings, there is no end of complaints about unproductive workers with long service who are protected by union seniority agreements. These workers cannot be fired short of outright theft. Mere incompetence will not justify their removal. In practice, they can only be bought out, often at considerable cost, deflecting resources away from more productive employees. More generally, whenever retention is not a function of the joint decision of the employer and employee, longer tenure is likely to be correlated with reduced productivity. Rapid turnover can be highly desirable if it stems from the ability to remove unproductive workers and leads to promoting able people within the firm, whose advance might be otherwise stifled.

Aggregate data on turnover cannot decide what mix a business needs of fresh blood and seasoned hands. The one point that is certain, however, is that union contracts do a poor job of sorting out which relationships, regardless of their duration, make sense and which do not. So long as there is no lock-step progression between length of service and productivity, management control over hiring, firing, promotion, and work rules is essential. The acid test lies not in the speculations of academic economists or lawyers. It rests in countless illustrations that unionized firms, burdened with probationary and seniority restrictions, often cannot compete with nonunionized firms that have greater flexibility in assembling and deploying their workforces. The upstart trucking companies that entered the market after the deregulation of surface transportation in 1980 decimated the ranks of the union competition whose entrenched wage structure and job rules made those firms unsustainable.[42] Seniority did not stave off new entrants, and the only

---

42. Michael H. Belzer, Collective Bargaining after Deregulation: Do the Teamsters Still Count? 48 Indus. & Lab. Rel. Rev. 636 (1995).

established firms that survived had to make the treacherous transition from a union to a nonunion shop.

A consistent theme among union supporters is that unions are necessary to counteract a management team that is mute and unresponsive. But by the same token it seems clear that management tasks are so difficult because they require a delicate balancing act. In this environment, it must be stressed that firing some workers is a necessary part of the job, for the optimal workplace environment can never be created by using all carrots and no sticks. That said, able managers do not make their decisions to dismiss in ignorance of workplace dynamics, but with full awareness of how these decisions are likely to play out. Often, some workers must be let go to protect productive workers from their less diligent colleagues. Employee dismissals are always a big deal even if they expose the employer to no legal liability whatsoever, as is the case under an at-will contract. No single worker operates in a void. Reputation and morale matter. Other workers have insecurities and start to look elsewhere if they think that the firing is unjustified. Potential applicants will decide that it is not worthwhile to work for the Queen of Hearts if decapitation is the response to revealing one's true preferences. In order to forestall these negative effects, dismissal is often accompanied with a severance package, even in the absence of any legal duty to provide one.

Pro-union scholars such as Freeman and Medoff buy into an inaccurate parody of labor relations in unregulated firms which claims that any union presence has to improve relationships in the workplace. Once recruitment, retention, and promotion are understood to be the lifeblood of the firm, this ostensible benefit of unionization disappears, for now the prospective worker has to make judgments not only about the firm but about the union. To be sure, some firms do not have enlightened managers. But in a competitive market those firms pay a real price. Non-wage terms matter, and the firm that does not do right by its employees will

not attract or retain the most productive workers. Decisions of productive workers to quit pose a huge threat to most firms, and the
effectiveness of the firm response does not depend on unions, but
on agile and sensitive managers.

The only interesting question left is how pro-union scholars
can be so off-base on their views of how ordinary firms work. The
most plausible explanation rests on their deep confusion between
legal doctrine and a firm's social practices. The implicit assumption is that so long as a firm has the power to hire and fire at will,
it is sure to use that power in an arbitrary fashion. Why caprice
works to the firm's advantage is left unstated. But the clear contrast is to a regulated regime such as that created under the labor
statutes in which workers can only be dismissed for well-
documented cause. That very formulation of the employment
relationship carries with it the patina of institutional reasonable-
ness that is not found in the dominant common-law rule on labor
contracts—the contract at will. [43] These at-will agreements provide that a worker can be fired for good reason, bad reason, or no
reason at all. On the other side, it is offset by the similar right of
at-will employees to leave at any time for any reason, good or
bad. That standard appears to enshrine mutual arbitrariness as a
preferred social norm. That impression is strengthened by vivid
examples of individual employers that act in an arbitrary and
high-handed fashion. Ironically, less reference is made about the
employees whose quitting leaves an employer in the lurch.

It is a mistake to concentrate on isolated examples at the expense
of the standard practice. The major flaw of the standard critique of
the at-will rule misapprehends how businesses and workers commonly operate under that rule. The sensible defense of the at-will
regime starts with the simple proposition that arrangements that

43. For my defense, *see* Richard A. Epstein, *In Defense of the Contract at Will* 51 U. Chi.
L. Rev. 947 (1984).

endure for long periods of time in all sorts of divergent labor markets must rest on a sound economic and social foundation. Otherwise it would be in the interest of all parties to switch voluntarily to some alternative regime. A little reflection reveals the hidden strengths of the rule. The first one is simple, in stark contrast to a union environment. Contracts at will are cheap to administer and generate little or no litigation. Of course, workers can sue for back wages. But they cannot treat any forward-looking decision on dismissal or demotion as a legally cognizable wrong. Before the introduction of the statutory schemes of workers' compensation, they could also sue for personal injuries, subject to a defense of assumption of risk, which chiefly was relevant in the case of open and obvious, but not latent, conditions. Similarly, the employer can sue a worker for the theft of trade secrets or the willful destruction of property. But no employer can insist that any worker remain in the company's employ. In all situations, additional contract provisions can provide that the employment relationship can continue for a specified term, with severance damages if these provisions are not honored—or even if they are. The at-will rule is a background or default norm, not an inexorable command. It helps create a legal regime with high flexibility and low administrative costs.

The at-will rule does not glorify the right of employers to take out latent hostilities or irrational ambitions on their hapless employees. It is better understood as a position that courts should not intervene in hiring and firing decisions, any more than they intervene in employee decisions to reject job offers or to quit. It is not possible through the legal process to capture the needed information to make intelligent judgments case by case, when context counts for so much. Nor is there any reason to do so, because the worker is protected by the quit option. The at-will rule has complete formal symmetry, because the options that it affords employees to go elsewhere, anywhere, and at any time, offer a strong restraint against employer opportunism. The workers who quit may have received better offers before they left. Understood in its rich context, the durability of the contract at will depends on its desirable incentive effects and the workplace environment it creates for all parties. Union defenders are wrong to think that the rule offers a license for arbitrary employer behavior. Market and reputational forces supply strong checks and balances against abusive employer behavior. Employers that seek to take advantage of workers will be met by a credible quit threat: why stay if the job promises no net benefit? Employers that fire arbitrarily will suffer reputational losses in the eyes of their other employees that will make it more difficult for them to hire and retain new employees. The firm's competitive position will erode with the decline in its performance. The incentives for good behavior exert a powerful hold on the managers and owners of nonunionized firms.

It is perfectly consistent with the contract at will for individual firms to develop internal sets of social norms that operate as a de facto "for cause" regime, where it is understood that dismissal will not be arbitrarily imposed. In most small firms, a workplace code emerges from close interaction that shapes shared social norms. Larger firms cannot rely exclusively on these forces, but must supplement them with formal review and grievance procedures that help them to rationalize their personnel decisions. Without those rules it becomes far more difficult to maintain a sense of parity among the workers, to clarify expectations on mutual rights and responsibilities and, in the current environment, to protect against employment discrimination lawsuits. Orientation sessions, firm outings, and team-building sessions are part of the workplace environment for a reason. A successful business finds it critical to foster positive relationships in order to create strong morale and to match workers with tasks that best match their interests and abilities.

Yet the key feature throughout is that this second tier of social norms does not, *by design*, create any legal obligations between the parties. Thus it is virtually standard today for large firms to prepare employer handbooks to provide an extensive set of protocols for internal use, all of which are prefaced by the explicit disclaimer in bold type that none of these obligations is judicially enforceable.[44] And smaller firms that dispense with the same level of formality will typically communicate the same consistent message to their employees.

This two-tier regime makes powerful economic and social sense. Freeman and Medoff wrongly ignore how unionization undermines this two-tier at-will environment by throwing obstacles in the path of employers that seek to create their own informal governance structures. For example, the ability of employers to foster these constructive interactions is frustrated by the outdated NLRA prohibition against company unions found in section 8(a)(2) that blocks the formation of employer-sponsored in-house operations. One key effect of this provision is that it casts a pall of uncertainty over any employer that wishes to meet directly with its workers, even in the absence of a union. These committees normally do not generate any difficulty when no union organization drive is in motion. But the moment that becomes a possibility, it is a litigation question whether these connections involve company-dominated labor organizations in violation of section 8(a)(2), on which there is naturally no clear line.[45] The efforts of employers to open up lines of communication are thus frustrated by the NLRA, which is far more concerned with giving the whip hand to a potential union representative who has commenced an organization campaign.

Section 8(a)(2) is commonly defended on the ground that the displacement of company-sponsored unions is needed to create

---

44. Natalie Bucciarelli Pedersen, *A Subjective Approach to Contracts?: How Courts Interpret Employee Handbook Disclaimers* (May 12, 2008) (Working Paper, *available* at http://papers.ssrn.com/sol3/papers.cfm?abstract_id=1132346).

45. On which, contrast NLRB v. Streamway Division, Scott & Fetzer Co., 691 F.2d 288 (6th Cir. 1982) (finding that no ULP existed when management/worker committees were established only for limited purposes, when workers acted in an individual and not a representative capacity) with Electromation, Inc., 309 NLRB 990 (1992), *enforced* 35 F.3d 1148 (7th Cir. 1994) (holding that employee "action committees" formed to combat dissatisfaction in the employer's unilateral wage changes violated §8(a)(2)).

breathing space for "authentic" unions.[46] But in practice that provision has profound anticompetitive effects by hampering efforts of firms to develop internal mechanisms that improve workplace relationships. It is not uncommon for unions to challenge the activities of various employer-employee committees as disguised company unions, especially in the heat of an organizing campaign. The use of the at-will contract is always compromised because the NLRA makes it an unfair labor practice to take any steps "to encourage or discourage membership in any labor organization,"[47] including dismissal for organizing activities. The moment the legal system creates a breach in the overall at-will environment, it forces firms to strengthen their formal systems of dispute resolution by making their "for-cause" environment legally binding, chiefly for the defensive purpose of avoiding statutory liability. In practice, they must offer reasons for the dismissal that negate any charge of an unfair labor practice. Remove the current threat of a ULP and the communications that Freeman and Medoff think unlikely will surely flourish.

In sum, the legal and social techniques available to nonunionized firms are sufficient to deal with all issues of internal management. There are no public goods or employment relations problems that labor unions solve for employers. It is no mystery why employers show routine resistance to labor organization. The current law forces them into relationships from which they can only receive a smaller slice of a smaller pie. EFCA will only exacerbate what is already a difficult situation for unionized firms. Many theorists think that the economic costs of unionization are justified by the democratic institutions it fosters. But that rationale is not available when direct worker participation in the recognition of a union is cut off by the card-check system, and direct worker ratification or

---

46. *See, e.g.*, Brudney II, supra at 19, "[I]n adopting §8(a)(2), Congress was focused on the more narrow issue of the need to eliminate in-house employer-dominated labor organizations in order to permit the growth of authentic collective bargaining."

47. NLRA, §8(a)(3).

rejection of a proposed master contract is blocked by mandatory "first contract" arbitration. Large numbers of workers will have *no say* in the arrangements that will bind them under a new statute that repudiates the proposition that the union should work for its members. With card-check and "first contract" arbitration, many workers will have no say in the arrangements that guide and organize their lives. These twin institutions will generate economic and social repercussions that are sure to spread throughout the system, leading to heightened workplace tensions and reduced job creation. No rational employer should be pleased with a smaller slice of a still smaller pie. The strong opposition to unions that many firms display is fully warranted by the economic facts on the ground.

THIRD PARTY EFFECTS: A CONSTANT SHARE OF A SMALLER PIE—AT BEST

The final piece of the EFCA puzzle requires some review of the overall effects of EFCA on society. These can be divided into three parts: allocative effects, distributional consequences, and disruption and dislocation.

Allocative Effects

The previous two sections have shown that the introduction of the original NLRA in 1935 shrank the size of the pie available to employers and employees by imposing external restrictions that prevent the emergence of dynamic competitive markets. For these purposes, however, it is best to accept those losses as a necessary cost of the current social commitment toward unionization. But a commitment to EFCA does not follow from any endorsement of the status quo. EFCA is more intrusive in virtually all regards and thus amplifies the adverse effects of unionization on the employer/

employee relationship. These effects cannot be confined to union-ized firms that are currently subject to the direct supervision of the NLRB. Any firm that employs workers also operates in multiple roles in a myriad of commercial settings, with customers, suppliers, and lenders being the most prominent. The interactions with these third parties are sometimes subject to direct regulation under the NLRA. Whenever labor law prohibits a firm from subcontract-ing—or from altering its current production model using current workers—it not only makes the operation of the regulated firm less efficient than it would otherwise be, but it also imposes losses on potential trading partners who necessarily have fewer options in the market. The social losses from lost opportunities are not entirely offset by the less efficient relationships adopted in their place, for strategies of mitigation can only reduce, not eliminate, the losses.

Even in the absence of such direct prohibitions, a strong labor regime will influence the welfare of both suppliers and customers through the price mechanism. The lower output by the unionized firm implies that it will purchase fewer complementary goods and services from its suppliers. On the other side, it will also ship fewer goods or render a smaller level of services to third persons, which are again sources of social loss. The reduced level of activity can make lending riskier, and thus can reduce the capital stock available to the firm. These indirect losses are likely to ripple broadly across society, which makes it difficult to assert that any particular group of third persons will bear the brunt of these losses. But second-order losses incurred by a larger number of firms and their employ-ees could easily add up to substantial social losses.

The presence of strong unions also has adverse consequences on nonunion workers by reducing their opportunities for employment and advancement, both in the unionized firm and in the countless other firms that do proportionately less business in consequence of unionization. In many cases the jobs lost are entry-level positions. This reduces opportunities for upward social mobility to the most vulnerable segments of the population, shutting them out of chances to join the middle class. In addition, the threat of instant unionization will retard the formation of the greatest driver of new jobs—small businesses—which are ill-equipped to deal with unionization at the riskiest stage of their business lives. Why try to form a business if labor negotiations could divert time and energy from product development and marketing operations? These losses multiply over time, for first jobs can lead to second jobs with greater prospects, better skills, and higher wages. EFCA will surely intensify these negative effects.

On the other side of the ledger, it is common for union supporters to claim that the constant threat of unionization induces employers to offer higher wages to workers, which they claim counts as a positive spillover from union activities to nonunion members. Thus Shaiken trumpets unions as "the folks that brought you the middle class," as if the multiple other sources of productivity from education to better infrastructure had nothing to do with it. Now the claim is this: "As union membership slides, however, both unions' ability to raise wages for their members and spin-off benefits for nonunion workers erode, wiping out the middle class dreams of many Americans."[48] In his view, unions in effect set the standard of living for others.

This argument is incorrect on both empirical and theoretical grounds. To start with the former, it would be useful to find some evidence of system-wide gains to back up this claim. All of the gross measures of labor productivity, however, coalesce around a single point: the greater the extent of unionization the lower the levels of productivity. In the United States, it is hard to test this proposition at the federal level given the uniform imposition of federal law. But it is possible to draw statewide comparisons that capture differences in union regulations or union penetration. To be sure, these tables are often confounded by other variables that might influence local rates of growth and income; taxation policy is one obvious factor.

---

48. *See* Shaiken *supra* note 3, at 4.

But on this question it is likely that states with strong union environments are likely to have other features that inhibit growth, such as high sales and income taxes. Notwithstanding the methodological caveats, the gross figures are vivid enough to call for an explanation by the defenders of unionization.

One key difference in state labor environments is state's right-to-work laws, which limit the influence of unionization. Here the evidence seems clear that states with these laws do on average better than those who do not. One study by William T. Wilson of the Mackinac Center for Public Policy found that right-to-work states have lower levels of unionization and higher rates of growth.[49] It was no surprise that Michigan experienced a growth rate in the market value of its goods and services of 1.8 percent during the period 1977 to 1999, relative to an average growth rate of 3.4 percent for right-to-work states. The same story is told with respect to growth in employment rates, where Michigan stood at 1.5 percent for the period between 1970 and 2000, while right-to-work states grew more significantly at 2.9 percent, or close to double that rate. The magnitude of these differences should not be underestimated because of the importance of compound interest. Over a twenty-year period, differential growth rates like these translate to about a 32 percent difference in employment levels between Michigan and right-to-work states. Figures like this are always elusive because they do not control for a wide range of other economic factors that could influence the overall level of growth, including high tax rates and emigration of Michigan residents to other states with better economic environments. That said, I am aware of no data that point in the opposite direction. Nor am I aware of any theoretical explanation that could reverse the clear implications from these findings, or those in other studies that have also correlated a rise in unionization with an increase in unemployment levels, which rests

49. William T. Wilson, *The Effect of Right to Work Laws on State Economic Development*, Mackinac Center Report, June 2002. *Available at* http://www.mackinac.org/archives/2002/s2002–02.pdf.

on the simple proposition that employers will offer fewer jobs when constrained to pay higher wages.[50] For example, Layne-Farrar in her review of the Canadian data notes that a 1 percent increase in union density raises the (lagged) unemployment rate by around 0.30,[51] which means that "if union density were to return to its 1995 level of 14.9 percent, a relatively modest gain of just under seven percentage points, the U.S. unemployment rate would increase by 0.83 − 0.99 percentage points."[52]

The same basic story is told when attention is turned to levels of union penetration, regardless of right-to-work laws. As these rates of unionization become higher, the overall level of employment growth slows down.[53] Hudson Institute Fellow Diana Furchtgott-Roth's figures indicate that the ten most heavily unionized states had lower rates of growth than the ten least unionized states. The growth rate of 2.77 percent for the unionized states varied between 24.6 percent and 19.6 percent union penetration. For the bottom ten states, the same numbers were a growth rate of 5.39 percent for states whose unionization levels varied between 3.3 percent and 5.9 percent. In fact, the differences are even more dramatic than these gross statistics suggest. Two of the three most heavily unionized states in the United States are Hawaii (number one) at 24.7 percent, and a growth rate of 11 percent, and Alaska (number three) at 22.2 percent with an 8.7 percent growth rate, both thinly populated states. The other eight states are New York, New Jersey, Washington, Michigan, Illinois, Minnesota, California, and Connecticut. When the growth rates are computed on this group that figure

50. *See, e.g.,* John DiNardo and David S. Lee, Economic Impacts of New Unionization on Private Sector Employers: 1984–2001, Q. J. Econ. 119 (2004): 1384–1441.

51. Anne Layne-Farrar, An Emprical Asessment of the Employee Free Choice Act: The Economic Implications 27 (2009)(SSRN etc.): [R]aising union density today by one standard deviation (7.28 percentage points) would raise the unemployment rate next year by about 2.20 percentage points (i.e., 7.28 x 0.30).

52. *Id.* at 28.

53. Diana Furchtgott-Roth, *Improving Union Financial Transparency*, Hudson Institute, Center for Employment Policy, *available at* http://hudson.org/files/pdf_upload/Union PaperAugust2907.pdf.

tumbles to 1 percent exactly, off a far larger population base. There are no similar surprises in the bottom ten states, all of which have positive rates, and only one of which, Mississippi, had a 1 percent growth rate, or the average for the large industrial states. It does not take much imagination to conclude that the states with the heaviest union populations had the worst experience. These numbers are hardly consistent with any story that claims that unions have propelled large numbers of individuals into the middle class.

These results are consistent with the broad outlines of general economic theory. It is critical to identify the supposed source of gains that propel some workers and their families into the middle class. Consider this common contention in favor of unionization: "Even modest increases in the share of the unionized labor force push wages upward, because non-unionized workplaces must keep up with unionized ones that collectively bargain for increases."[54] But why should nonunion firms follow suit? Let one firm raise the rates to its existing workers, and the number of workers employed at that firm, all other things being equal, will decline. The excess workers are still available to rival firms, who are now able to offer lower wages because of the increase in the supply of available workers. These firms know, moreover, that the lower wages will translate into lower prices, which give them a competitive edge that a union firm is not likely to match, especially if its work rules inhibit productivity gains by reducing flexibility in operations. Workers, moreover, will flock to these rival firms for the reasons mentioned above. The competitive success of nonunionized companies creates opportunities for expansion that redound to their benefit. The basic truth remains: in the long run, sustainable wage increases are tied to higher levels of productivity that union work rules and other restrictive practices in general thwart.

This analysis remains valid when we focus exclusively on the

54. Editorial, The Labor Agenda, N.Y. Times, Dec. 29, 2008, at A 22.

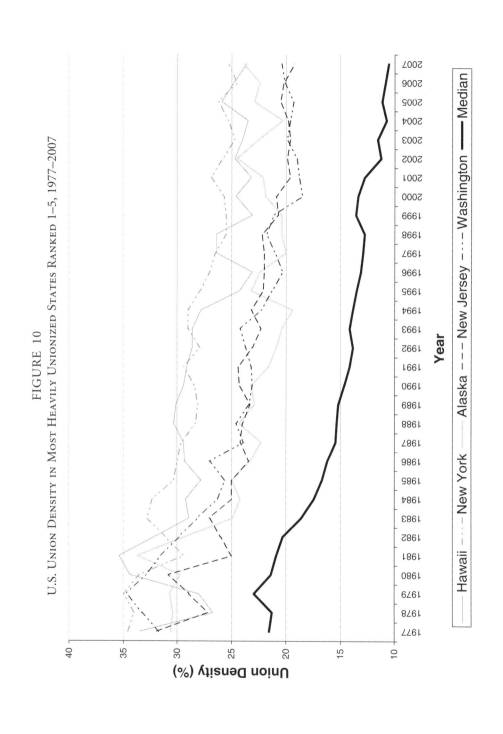

FIGURE 10

U.S. UNION DENSITY IN MOST HEAVILY UNIONIZED STATES RANKED 1–5, 1977–2007

— New York —— Alaska – – New Jersey – · – Washington —— Median
—— Hawaii – · · –

Year

Union Density (%)

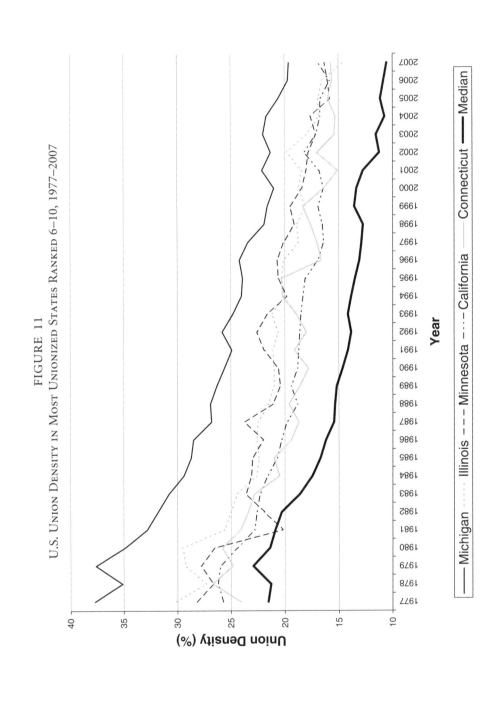

FIGURE 11

U.S. UNION DENSITY IN MOST UNIONIZED STATES RANKED 6–10, 1977–2007

Union Density (%)

Year

——— Michigan ·········· Illinois – – – Minnesota – · – California ——— Connecticut ——— Median

TABLE 7

UNION DENSITY AND JOB GROWTH FOR SOME STATES

State	Percentage Unionized	Job Growth % Increase 2001–2006*
Hawaii	24.70%	11.00%
New York	24.40%	0%
Alaska	22.20%	8.70%
New Jersey	20.10%	1.90%
Washington	19.80%	6.00%
Michigan	19.60%	-4.80%
Illinois	16.40%	-1.00%
Minnesota	16.00%	2.70%
California	15.70%	3.20%
Connecticut	15.60%	0%
Rhode Island	15.30%	3.10%
Wisconsin	14.90%	1.60%
South Dakota	5.90%	5.40%
Mississippi	5.60%	1.00%
Utah	5.40%	11.20%
Florida	5.20%	9.10%
Arkansas	5.10%	4.00%
Texas	4.90%	5.70%
Georgia	4.40%	4.00%
Virginia	4.00%	5.90%
North Carolina	3.30%	3.20%
South Carolina	3.30%	.40%

*Id. Table 16, at 60

unionized firm. All too often, the increased wages of union members come at the expense of other workers in the unionized firms, which exacerbates income differentials, just as Milton Friedman observed long ago.[55] Freeman and Medoff recognize the force of this claim, but dispute its implications by insisting that unions create greater parity of wages within firms—without acknowledging the inefficiencies that this parity can create.[56] These intra-firm wage alterations do not have any allocative effects, either positive or negative; whatever one side gains is offset by losses on the other side.

---

55. Milton Friedman, *Capitalism and Freedom* 124 (University of Chicago Press 1963).
56. Freeman & Medoff *supra* note 2, at 16.

What matters is the market structure in which the wage adjustments take place. And wage and benefit increases will prove sustainable only if they are supported by sufficient increases in worker productivity. Here, as a first approximation, the social effects of wage increases should be negative if they result from monopolization of the workplace. And they are equally unfortunate if they lead employers to offer monopoly wages to others in order to stave off union organization.

Even if these wage increases were regarded as an unalloyed social good, this defense of unionization still fails. The simplest point in response is that the threat of unionization is not simply met by raising the wage levels to present employees. Rather, the inability to stave off unionization once the plant is up and running generates multiple responses, of which wage increases are only one. The key insight is that the threat of unionization induces nonunionized firms to make other socially wasteful decisions solely for defensive reasons. The location and design of plants are two decisions that are often altered to deflect the threat of unionization. Firms may locate plants in anti-union environments and automate them in ways that reduce dependency on a unionized force. Or better yet, they may go overseas with production that cannot be efficiently undertaken in the United States, costing jobs that could otherwise be kept at home. These negative impacts would be avoided if a firm knew that it could remain nonunion no matter where it located. But under the present law, the risk of unionization is borne by all firms, including those which have no union workers, which means that the labor statutes hurt the capital value of all firms. It follows that the differential rates of growth referred to above tell only part of the story. The full story requires taking into account the downward pressure that unionization imposes on all firms, unionized or not, which is hard to measure empirically.

The law in effect imposes a system-wide efficiency tax. For example, unions are vigorous opponents of global outsourcing, which they hope to defeat by a complex set of taxes and prohibitions, many of which could give an unintended boost to foreign firms with no American connections. The EFCA makes it possible for arbitrators to decree that result on a firm-by-firm basis (at the very least) which in turn creates the serious risk that these provisions will rapidly become the de facto standard for new contracts. The chilling effect of this position will be hard to isolate in individual cases, for it is not possible to interview the heads of firms that were never formed, or those that chose to organize off-shore from the beginning. But it is highly likely that the aggregate statistics on the formation of new businesses will reflect the EFCA's implicit tax on job creation. The key point to remember is that there is, going forward, no identity of interest between the unions which profit from EFCA and the workers whose job opportunities are limited by its passage. A far better strategy for helping workers is to opt for a more competitive labor environment at home. In the end, new job creation will swamp whatever distributional gains EFCA promises for some select group of workers. Increased coercion never leads to increased productivity. EFCA will surely exert an overall negative effect on the wages and job opportunities of employees.

These negative effects are aggravated by the political consequences of stronger union influence, which help explain the anemic, indeed nonexistent, growth rates in places like New York. Unions do not do well against competition from domestic or foreign firms without statutory protection, even on the dubious assumption that they somehow provide benefits to workers that the firms cannot supply for themselves. The rapid rise of unions in the United States started in the New Deal period. This success depended not only on the political willingness to provide unions with key structural protections in the form of exclusive bargaining rights for all members of the bargaining unit. It depended heavily on complementary social institutions that fostered monopoly industries, such as the unified AT&T, which were also insulated from competition.[57] It is much harder for unions to survive, let alone prosper, in a competitive business environment. But today's current competitive environment is not written in stone. In the eyes of the Supreme Court, our constitutional order does not attach any priority to competition over state-protected monopolies.[58] It is possible for the government to sponsor cartels on Monday and subject them to criminal prosecution on Tuesday, which is what happened in the regulation of domestic oil production in the United States in the 1930s.[59] The absence of any priority in favor of competition over monopoly invites not only the passage of EFCA, but also a retrograde curtailment in international and domestic free-trade policies in order to recreate the corporatist environment that allowed unions to thrive (and others to suffer) in the wake of the New Deal initiatives of the 1930s.

Unions have to compete in the political environment with a myriad of business, religious, academic, agricultural, and political interests. No one has a monopoly of influence over the legislative process or the public debate. But for all the political competition they face, labor unions have done well in gaining protections against nonunion workers and firms not only under the labor law, but also through protective tariffs, minimum wage laws, and other statutes, such as the Davis-Bacon Act, which requires prevailing (i.e., union) wages to be paid on all public works projects funded by the federal government.[60] On the domestic front, unions take

57. *See,* Michael Wachter, Labor Unions: A Corporatist Institution in a Competitive World, 155 U. Pa. L. Rev. 581, 609 (2007): "Although the strongest supporters of regulation had always been AT&T and the labor unions, it was believed to have strong public support as well. When AT&T settled and agreed to a deregulation plan under Judge Harold Greene [in 1982], there was no longer much public support for cartel-like regulatory systems."

58. For a clear statement of the preference, *see* Robert Stern, The Commerce Clause and the National Economy, 59 Harv. L. Rev. 645 (1946).

59. *See* United States v. Socony-Vacuum Oil Co., 310 U.S. 150 (1940). For an account *see* Daniel A. Crane, *The Story of* United States v. Socony-Vacuum: *Hot Oil and Antitrust in the Two New Deals, in* Antitrust Stories 91 (Eleanor M. Fox & Daniel A. Crane eds., 2007).

60. The Davis-Bacon Act (40 U.S.C. §§ 276a—276a-5).

strong activist positions on land use cases in order to prevent non-union firms from entering areas dominated by union firms. "Your zoning ordinance is the best weapon you have to stop Wal-Mart."[61] Likewise, on the international front, unions working hand-in-hand with their preferred employers will bring anti-dumping actions to harass foreign competitors.[62]

The magnitude of these union efforts is directly dependent on the financial base and the political chits that unions collect. It is no accident that union members are the single largest interest group represented at the Democratic National Convention, or that unions are conspicuously large contributors to Democrats' political campaigns.[63] When SEIU gave its resounding endorsement to Obama, Stern made clear the reason why: "There has never been a fight in Illinois or a fight in the nation where our members have not asked Barack Obama for assistance and he has not done everything he could to help us." [64] And, of course, as a senator, Obama was one of the sponsors of EFCA, and has promised to sign it as president, as stated on the SEIU Web site.[65]

61. *See* Wal-Mart Watch, http://walmartwatch.com/battlemart/go/cat/zoning_regulations. SEIU is the "principal funder" of the site. http://walmartwatch.com/blog/archives/seiu_and_wal_mart/.

62. *See e.g.*, Final Ruling Fails to Surprise, China Daily, Apr. 20, 2004, discussing how two labor unions and a TV manufacturer worked together in a case before the Department of Commerce against Chinese firms dumping TVs in the U.S. market.

63. At the 2008 Democratic National Convention, over 1,000 (25%) of the delegates were "active or retired union members or union household members." Seth Michaels, *Union Members 25 Percent of Democratic Convention Delegates*, Aug. 21, 2008, *available at* http://blog.aflcio.org/2008/08/21/union-members-25-percent-of-democratic-convention-delegates.

64. Jesse J. Holland, Powerful 1.9M-Member Union Backs Obama, Huffington Post, Feb. 15, 2008, *available at* http://www.huffingtonpost.com/2008/02/15/powerful-19m member-unio ...n_86860.html.

65. http://www.seiu.org/employeefreechoice/ (featured video), visited December 24, 2008. "If a majority of workers in a company want a union, they should get a union. It's that simple." But of course it is not. Obama's endorsement makes no mention that majority will has been the rule under the NLRA since 1935, and refers to neither the card-check nor the compulsory interest arbitration features that make the bill so controversial.

Distributional Consequences

Another element of the picture that needs to be addressed is the distributional consequences of EFCA. This discussion takes place against a background of increased differential wealth in the United States. The sources of that difference are not easy to detect, but surely much of it has to do with the differential opportunities for education, which are of ever greater value in the information age. There is nothing that can be done through unionization to alter that distribution of power, for if the competitive wage falls for persons with little or no education, as it surely has in the past generation or so, the monopoly power of unionization starts from a lower base, which makes it unlikely that it could ever offset that decline, especially since the increased supply of nonunion workers poses at least some limitation on the power to raise these wages. Likewise, within limits it is always possible for government, especially at the federal level, to try to work a redistribution of wealth through taxation which is in general a more efficient way to handle the task because it does not create a gap between those workers lucky enough to gain from selective unionization relative to those who do not.[66] The earned income tax credit, for example, is an explicit tool that is addressed to this issue, which has more even distributional effects and smaller allocative losses.[67]

Yet for these purposes, the question is whether the passage of EFCA could by itself strengthen the position of the middle class. The argument in support of that claim rests on the view that the original NLRA did this seventy years ago. But there is no reason to think that this claim is true. The increase in incomes depends on an overall increase in productivity, which is more likely attributable

---

66. The same proposition applies to efforts to redistribute wealth by changing, as the NLRA does, contract terms between the parties. No matter what the incidence of the new liability, the losses will be shared by the two parties in some uncertain proportions. That party who has the more inelastic demand or supply will bear the brunt of the losses.

67. *See, e.g.,* Nada Essisa & Jeffrey Liebman, Labor Supply Response to the Earned Income Tax Credit,111 Q. J. Econ. 605, 605 (1996).

to innovation that expands the size of the pie—not union struggles that seek to alter its division. Even if EFCA does pass, there is no reason to think that its distributional effects will work an improvement on the lot of the middle class, given its persistent downward pressure on overall productivity. Large portions of the current middle class are not union members now and will not become union members after EFCA. They will bear the brunt of the statute and find their positions compromised. In addition, of course, union members and nonunion workers both are enrolled in pension plans whose value depends on the ability of corporations to continue to earn the dividends that support the share prices of the stocks in pension portfolios. These capital values will diminish, although no one can say by how much. Union members occupy multiple roles like all other citizens, and any gains that they might achieve in wages and benefits through EFCA are likely to be offset by the increased prices that they have to pay to obtain goods and services from a unionized Wal-Mart and by the loss of jobs offshore. The unionization of one firm does nothing to benefit union members of other groups. This pessimistic assessment is brutal but true. We cannot regulate our nation's labor markets to increase overall social wealth. The likely consequence of EFCA is to reduce income and employment across the board. The only unknown concerns the size of the loss, which will depend in part on the administrative regulations and judicial decisions needed to fill in EFCA's very substantial gaps. No one knows whether the actions of interstitial lawmaking will mitigate or inflame the errors. No one should support the passage of a statute that holds out such political risks.

Disruption and Dislocation

My last point is that EFCA necessarily introduces a large measure of instability that could lead to bitter negotiations and disappointed expectations all around. Let the arbitral system be weighted in favor of the union claim, and one of two things will happen. If the arbitration arrangement is carried forward, it will lead to contraction of business or bankruptcy, which itself becomes a source of tension. If the arbitration system does not carry over, it is highly likely that an employer will resist the continuation of an employment relationship that he did not consent to in the first place. Either way, we can be confident that unrest in labor relations will increase, at a time when the economy is likely to suffer from a general slowdown. White House Chief of Staff Rahm Emanuel has said that it is a shame to let a good crisis go to waste.[68] His point was that major economic reversals can lead to major reforms. But his is a high-risk strategy, for the *wrong* reform program is likely to generate worse consequences in bad times than in good times.

---

68. *See Rahm Emanuel on the Opportunities of Crisis*, video on The Wall Street Journal Online, 11/18/2008, *available at* http://online.wsj.com/video/rahm-emanuel-on-the-opportunities-of-crisis/3F6B98 80-D1FD-492B-9A3D-70DBE8EB9E97.html.

CHAPTER 4
CONSTITUTIONAL IMPLICATIONS

The bulk of this analysis of EFCA is directed at its impact on workers, employers, and the overall economy. The radical transformation that EFCA promises is sure to raise significant challenges to the constitutionality of its key provisions on card check and interest arbitration. The initial assumption of most modern scholars is that since the 1937 constitutional revolution,[1] Congress enjoys carte blanche on the types of programs that it can pass in the economic sphere, so that any detailed analysis is wholly beside the point. That assumption is no doubt correct with respect to ordinary legislation. But EFCA is no ordinary statute. It has such expansive ambitions that the facile presumption of its constitutionality is unwarranted. Indeed, even under the lax standards of current law, powerful and focused constitutional challenges raise serious considerations based on rights of speech and association. Following is an account of the two most vulnerable portions of the current statute, the card check and the interest arbitration, separately and in tandem.

THE CARD CHECK

The secretive and coercive nature of the card-check system infringes the ordinary rights of political association that are guaranteed to

---

1. *See* NLRB v. Jones & Laughlin Steel Co., 301 U.S. 1 (1937), upholding the original Wagner Act against all challenges.

workers, and perhaps their employers, under the First Amendment. The words of Justice Harlan are instructive:

> It is beyond debate that freedom to engage in association for the advancement of beliefs and ideas is an inseparable aspect of the "liberty" assured by the Due Process Clause of the Fourteenth Amendment, which embraces freedom of speech. Of course, it is immaterial whether the beliefs sought to be advanced by association pertain to political, economic, religious, or cultural matters, and state action which may have the effect of curtailing the freedom to associate is subject to the closest scrutiny.[2]

The key justification for the 1935 Wagner Act was that its rejection of the common-law system of individual voluntary agreements still left workers with rights to full participation in the selection of unions by secret ballot (after hearing employer speech) and in the ratification of labor contracts by a vote of all bargaining unit members. The simple logic on this legal transformation was that these democratic mechanisms offered a sufficient quid pro quo for the loss of individual associational rights, given the added power that workers could obtain with a union as their exclusive bargaining representative. The vote on both the union and the contract is gone under the EFCA for the initial representation period, so the question is whether the act offers substitute protections that justify the abridgement of these associational freedoms for dissident workers who have no rights of expression at either stage of the process.

The First Amendment issues here are knotty. Under current law, concerns with coercion and free expression lie behind the uniform line of First Amendment Supreme Court cases that deal with the relationship of individual workers to the union. For the most part these issues have been relatively narrow in scope, given the ability of all workers to participate in the selection of the union and the

---

2. *See, e.g.*, NCAAP v. Alabama, 357 U.S. 449, 460–61 (1958) (using associational freedoms to keep NAACP membership lists out of the hands of the Alabama attorney general).

ratification of its contracts. One common issue is the extent to which union dues can be used not just to "defray the expenses of the negotiation or administration of collective agreements, or the expenses entailed in the adjustment of grievances and disputes,"[3] but also to advance the political agenda of the union, which may espouse causes to which dissident members of the unions are opposed. These cases raise conflicts between two strong values. The first is that each individual worker should be entitled to a range of autonomy that does not require him to support views with which he disapproves. Each should be protected by a constitutional rule that no union election can force that worker to support political expression to which he is opposed. On the other side, nonunion members should not be allowed a free ride from union efforts to create benefits for them. The perception that each union creates a limited public good is used to justify the ability of unions to tax nonmembers for their contributions to the common plan.

The tension between these two values is a reflection of the current issues in democratic politics. Individuals may have to live with elected officials, and they must pay their fair share of taxes in order to support the common activities of the state, lest they become "free riders" who derive material benefits from government activities to which they make no contribution. But their allegiance is limited in light of the First Amendment guarantees of freedom of speech. In particular, dissident citizens do not have to contribute their money or labor to successful political campaigns of their adversaries in order to entrench the incumbents. The standard First Amendment protection for political action balances the fears of free riding on the collective against the risk of majority domination.

These same considerations are very much in play in the union context. The law allows unions to collect dues to support the business activities of the unions but not their political participation,

---

3. *See* IAM v. Street, 367 U.S. 740, 768 (1961).

which is in the tens of millions of dollars.[4] The line between these business and political expenditures is not always clear, but the critical 1988 Supreme Court decision in *Communications Workers v. Beck*[5] sought to classify the various types of expenditures. Union conventions, social activities, and publications could be financed with dues collected from dissenting workers so long as they did not directly fund political activities. But organizing activities outside the bargaining unit did not qualify.

The central challenge is to determine how this reconciliation between controlling free riding and preserving individual autonomy carries over to the new environment created by EFCA's card-check and compulsory arbitration provisions. In dealing with this question, it is difficult to know exactly what standard of review should be given. Within the framework of the current NLRA, Congress receives considerable deference because of the institutional safeguards to worker autonomy from political participation. But these rights are stripped away from dissenting workers who could be forced into a union without their knowledge or their participation. Perhaps the level of constitutional scrutiny for this substantial infringement of individual rights of autonomy may be judged on a lower standard than for the loss of political rights covered under both *Street* and *Beck*. But it would be a mistake to draw any hard line that treats the EFCA as having only economic but not political significance, given that participation in union democracy has, almost by definition, a significant political component.

The peculiar status of labor unions may weigh heavily against applying strict scrutiny to these prohibitions on participation in either the selection of the union or the ratification of the first contract. We know that the rules on freedom of speech in union campaigns give a broader account to the meaning of coercion in union

---

4. According to www.unionfacts.com, in 2007 National Educational Association reported spending $32 million and California Teachers Association spent $58 million on political activities. In an article in Seattle *Post Intelligencer* from October 17, 2006, Richard Berman reports that "labor's political expenditures totaled $925 million in the 2004 cycle."

5. *See* Commun. Workers of Amer. v. Beck, 487 U.S. 735 (1988).

settings than elsewhere.[6] But they certainly do not eviscerate all First Amendment considerations, so it is appropriate to rely on judicial review to examine the justifications offered for this loss of the worker rights that are part economic and part political.

The best view seems to impose on the government some standard of intermediate scrutiny, which requires that it show how the restrictions on participation in critical bargaining unit activities serve some substantial public end by means reasonably appropriate to the task. At this point, the only justifications put forward are partisan, not social, insofar as the expansion of union penetration in the workplace is the desired end, not any independent measure of worker welfare. That skeptical account of EFCA is fortified because the statistical and anecdotal evidence put forward to explain why these restrictions are needed is unsound. These purported rationales fail on questions of both the desired ends and the means chosen to achieve them. On the first question, the only legitimate objective is the control of unfair labor practices by employees, for which—if the case were made out—the only needed remedy would be the provisions that increase the sanctions that are imposed on employers who commit ULPs during organization campaigns. But so long as the increased sanctions are available under Section 3, there is no reason to completely transform the entire structure of labor law through the card-check system coupled with compulsory interest arbitration. Worse still, the means here are far too broad for any supposed end. The evidence presented about widespread employer abuse is flawed from the collection of the data to the interpretation of the results, removing the factual predicate of employer irregularities on which the card-check system must stand.

It will be argued that this result runs against the use of card checks throughout the legal system. But on this point it is clear that the constitutional scrutiny of legislation that allows Congress or

6. *See* the text of § 8(c), supra at 34, and NLRB v. Gissel Packing Co., 395 U.S. 575 (1969), supra at 26 note 9.

state legislatures to bind *themselves* is less than that which is used to determine whether they can impose similar restrictions on *private, nongovernmental* firms, just as the First Amendment scrutiny of public employees is less severe than it is of state restrictions on the speech rights of private employees.[7] Approving the card-check system for public employees does not require the same result for private employees. Indeed, the differences are still starker because of the peculiar imbalances in the card-check system that provide large openings for union coercion. Unions can prevent workers who have signed their union cards from changing their minds. Yet the law refuses to allow anti-union workers to make binding commitments to oppose union representation. On this view, the card-check system would be unconstitutional even if the provisions for interest arbitration were struck from the statute. The card-check system has no clear legitimate end, and the means chosen clearly terminate the rights of workers to participation in union affairs, while forcing employers to deal with unions when they are denied all opportunity to make their case against the union. So long as worker participation is the key to upholding the limitations on common-law rights under the original Wagner Act, this card-check program exceeds constitutional limitations.

In response to my position first outlined in the *Wall Street Journal*,[8] Professor Michael Gottesman minimized this First Amendment objection to EFCA's design of the card-check system as "improbable." He concedes, as I think he must, that a flat-out ban on employer speech of unionization is constitutionally infirm.[9] But he continues by insisting that the lesser sanctions are constitutionally permissible.

> It's one thing to say that the government can't muzzle an employer from expressing its views. It's quite another to say that the

---

7. *See, e.g.*, Connick v. Meyers, 461 U.S. 138 (1983).

8. Richard A. Epstein, The Employee Free Choice Act Is Unconstitutional, The Wall Street Journal, December 19, 2008.

9. Michael Gottesman, The Improbable Claim That EFCA Is Unconstitutional, American Constitution Society, February 4, 2009.

government has to structure its laws to provide employers notice about when their speech might be most efficacious. Under EFCA, employers will remain free to voice their views about the downsides of unionization whenever and as often as they want. They can rail against unions on a continuing basis, so long as they refrain from threats or coercion. That's all the First Amendment guarantees them. Epstein's "advance notice" theory is unheard of in First Amendment jurisprudence, and would produce preposterous results. Consider just one example: under Epstein's theory, a court couldn't entertain a lawsuit by an employee against her employer unless she first notified the employer of her intention to sue, so that the employer would have an opportunity to express its views about the desirability of her bringing suit.

The weakness of this position should be evident at both a theoretical and practical level. On the first point, the employer's ability to "rail against unions" in the abstract ignores wholly the right of dissident workers to speak up on issues of vital concern to them. Why should they be bound by a procedure that does not allow them to speak? In addition, the innocent qualification that employers "refrain from threats or coercion" only takes its meaning from the peculiar labor law context which under section 8(c) gives a far broader account of coercion than is found anywhere else in First Amendment Law.

Most critically, within the framework of the current act, the employer is not in a tenable position solely because it is free to "rail against" unions in the abstract, without being able to tailor its remarks against a known adversary before the card check is a fait accompli. On this point, Gottesman's poorly constructed example of notice prior to litigation cuts *against* his position. The reason why no party has to give notice of its intention to sue before filing its claim is that the complaint itself gives notice of the plaintiff's theory of the case and request for relief, to which the defendant can then answer. But who would allow a complaint filed without notice to impose a binding judgment on the defendant? That notice is

strictly required on constitutional grounds today.[10] Yet that notice
is precisely what the secret card check denies the employer, who
has the right to respond *only* after it is bound under EFCA, not
before. It is easy enough to cure this fatal defect in the card-check
system by requiring notification of an intention to organize coupled
with a rule that validates only cards filed, say, ten days after that
date. The interest of the employer and dissident employees are
legitimate and large. The desire of the union to bypass the delibera-
tion process is manifest but illegitimate. Under the present regime,
it is not credible to prop up any government-imposed scheme that
rigs the rules so that binding decisions are made after only one side
has been heard.

Compulsory Interest Arbitration

EFCA's interest arbitration provisions are even more vulnerable to
constitutional attack. The initial but limited attack on the statute is
that it creates an impossibly broad delegation of lawmaking authority to the Federal Mediation and Conciliation Service, which can
constitute arbitral panels in whatever way it sees fit. Historically,
the rigid tripartite division of federal power into the legislative,
executive, and judicial branches made it difficult to accommodate
any system of delegation by the legislature to either the executive
or independent agencies. As Justice Story wrote, "The general rule
of law is, that a delegated power cannot be delegated."[11] The concerns that animated this doctrine were several. One was a fear that
it would remove key decisions from the system of political account-
ability set up under the Constitution. A second was that the delegated party would act in ways that moved the law beyond the
position that the legislature would adopt. There is some authority
that allows aggrieved parties to challenge broad statutory language

---

10. *See* Mullane v. Central Hannover Bank & Trust Co., 339 U.S. 306 (1950).
11. Shankland v. Washington, 30 U.S. 390, 395 (1831).

on the grounds that it permits their excessive delegation of legislative authority.[12] These concerns, however, have largely been overmatched by the need to create independent agencies like the NLRB—whose members can be removed by the president only with cause—to accommodate the vast expansion of government activity in the modern period.[13] Without question, the imperatives of the administrative state have made it exceedingly difficult in modern times to mount any sustained attack against standard-making under the non-delegation doctrine.[14] But in principle the nondelegation doctrine remains. Modern cases require at least some articulation of the end to be served so that they meet the modest test of showing some "intelligible principle," by which it can be determined whether the agency in question has complied with the sense of the statute.[15] But in this case the sketchy nature of the statute offers no clues about the many particular decisions that have to be addressed on the full range of arbitral questions. Striking it down on these grounds would not end the initiative, but would require Congress to do what it should have done already, which is to articulate some substantive boundaries on what arbitrators can and cannot do.

Worse is that the procedures chosen to implement this proposed statute invite a biased selection of arbitrators who can make decisions that are not reviewable on their merits by any independent party. It seems self-evident that EFCA will only pass with large political majorities from the Democratic side, which also controls all

12. *See, e.g.*, Schechter Poultry Corporation v. United States, 295 U.S. 495 (1935)(striking down broad delegation to private groups to set industrial standards); Amalgamated Meat Cutters v. Connally, 337 F. Supp. 737 (D.D.C. 1971) (upholding delegation of nationwide price and wage controls under the Economic Stabilization Act introduced to eliminate "gross inequities" in existing patterns).

13. *See, e.g.,* Humphrey's Executor v. United States, 295 U.S. 602 (1935).

14. *See* Whitman v. American Trucking Associations, Inc., 531 U.S. 457 (2001).

15. *Id.* at 472. (". . . we repeatedly have said that when Congress confers decision-making authority upon agencies Congress must 'lay down by legislative act an intelligible principle to which the person or body authorized to [act] is directed to conform'.")

appointments within the Department of Labor. Perhaps in the full-ness of time the regulations under EFCA will clearly articulate how the arbitral panels will be selected and organized and thus undercut the serious due process objections that relate to bias, the opportunity to be heard, vagueness, and the denial of any judicial review on the merits. On this ground too, Professor Gottesman defends the consti-tutionality of EFCA on grounds that only show its constitutional infirmity when he notes that "the system employed by the Federal Mediation and Conciliation Service (FMCS) for selection of arbitra-tors furnishing a list from which each party strikes names until only one name is left virtually guarantees that the lunatic arbitrator Epstein envisions will not be chosen."[16]

Lunacy is not a particularly high standard of constitutional pro-bity, especially when the employer has no option to exit the system. And, nothing in EFCA either requires or precludes the adoption of this system. But note its manifest weakness. Gottesman's remarks ignore the obvious objection that nothing constrains FMCS in its choice of names to put on the list. In an Obama administration, all of these could be from the labor side of a deep chasm, which is a palpable form of bias no matter what the arbitral panel says in mak-ing its decision. And it is cold comfort to note that "arbitrators determine terms and conditions by reference to what other employ-ers in the industry pay, the particular employer's financial situation, and other criteria." Therein lies the problem. In effect, the standards applied to one firm now bind all others, so that any form of compe-tition in internal organization is necessarily squelched by arbitrators who are entitled to make reference to inefficient business arrange-ments imposed on other firms. And it would be simply disastrous to engage in arbitral ratemaking that in looking at the "peculiar" position of a given firm could impose higher wages on firms without debt in their capital structure than on firms that do have debt in theirs—a view that has been struck down as unconstitutional in

16. Gottesman, id.

other rate regulation contexts.[17] Nor is there any comfort in allowing unspecified "other criteria" to play a decisive role. EFCA counts as the classic illustration where the supposed flexibility of the arbitral system simply opens the door to boundless discretion.

As characterized by EFCA's defenders, the inescapable level of discretion in choosing an arbitral panel does not meet the constitutional minimal standards of fair play under the Due Process Clause. To be sure, this is not a case where persons are subject to potential discharge or criminal sanctions, so that some flexibility may be in order. But by the same token, the creation of financial and other obligations stemming from these arbitrations could dwarf in magnitude the losses from the traditional types of administrative hearings to which due process protections can attach. It is also important to stress that the arbitral hearing under EFCA is not a form of administrative rule-making for which, generally speaking, no individual person gets special rights to be heard, given the broad number of participants in the process.[18] Nor in rule-making proceedings is it necessary to afford procedural protections that go beyond those specified in the Administrative Procedure Act of 1946[19] to meet the requirements of due process of law.[20] But compulsory arbitration is a form of adjudication in which the individual claims to be judged by known rules, administered by neutral judges. In these contexts, a "fair trial in a fair tribunal is a basic requirement of due process," in administrative proceedings as well as litigation.[21] In this case, the standardless rules for adjudication make

---

17. *See* Calfarm Insurance Co. v. Deukmejian, 771 P.2d 1247, 1254 (Cal. 1989), striking down, as a taking under the due process clause, a California initiative that allowed a rate increase before a particular date only to firms that showed a substantial threat of insolvency.

18. *See, e.g.,* Bi-Metallic Invest Co. v. State Board of Equalization, 239 U.S. 441 (1915). ("Where a rule of conduct applies to more than a few people it is impracticable that everyone should have a voice in its adoption.")

19. 5 U.S.C. §§ 551 et seq.

20. Vermont Yankee Nuclear Power Corp. v. Natural Resources Defense Council, Inc., 435 U.S. 519 (1978).

21. See In re Murchinson, 349 U.S. 133, 136 (1955), applied to cases of bias in administrative adjudications see Withrow v. Larkin, 421 U.S. 35 (1975).

it impossible for anyone to know whether a particular decision is right or wrong, let alone one which will plunge a firm into bankruptcy. The danger of bias is manifest.

But why run this risk? EFCA could have avoided both the appearance and likelihood of bias if it had simply provided for the appointment of a neutral arbitrator who did not answer directly to the head of FMCS, a political appointee. And the absence of any kind of judicial review in an Article III Court—i.e. those staffed with judges with tenure during good behavior and protection against salary reduction[22]—removes one of the key safeguards imposed in those cases in which "non-Article III" rulings have been held to be constitutional by the U.S. Supreme Court.[23] The claims for expedition remove the possibility that any independent eyes will see whether the agreement violates principles of fundamental fairness. It has already been held that the absence of judicial review can offend the norms of due process in cases where judicial review of a jury award was not allowed "unless the court can affirmatively say there is no evidence to support the verdict."[24] Supreme Court Justice John Paul Stevens held that absence of standard judicial review to challenges of excessive verdicts did not provide sufficient safeguards against "the danger of arbitrary awards."[25] The context may differ, but the risk is there. Defenders of EFCA could insist that speed is of the essence in these cases. That contention is odd in that there is no prescribed time for issuing the arbitral decree. And it is insufficient because it rules out expedited review which could act as an effective check on arbitral misconduct. These procedural defects

---

22. U.S. Const. Art. III, § 1: The Judges, both of the supreme and inferior Courts, shall hold their Offices during good Behaviour, and shall, at stated Times, receive for their Services, a Compensation, which shall not be diminished during their Continance in Office."

23. *See, e.g.,* Crowell v. Benson, 285 U.S. 22, 54 (1932). ("[T]he reservation of full authority to the court to deal with matters of law provides for the appropriate exercise of the judicial function in this class of cases [e.g. workers' compensation claims under the Longshoreman and Harborworkers Act]."

24. *See* Honda Motor Co. v. Oberg, 512 U.S. 415 (1994).

25. *Id.* at 432.

could in principle be cured by some modifications of EFCA. But as it stands, I know of no statutory or administrative scheme that offers so little process.

Making these due-process challenges will raise additional complications because there will also be a tendency in the courts to defer this challenge on the ground that it is not ripe until the regulations are adopted, and even then to postpone the challenge still further to see just how those regulations play out in practice. But this is one instance in which the penchant for "as applied" review on the structure of these panels is an open invitation to disaster, as there would be thousands of cases in various stages of arbitration or settlement before the regulations are promulgated, vetted through rule-making processes, or applied in an individual case. The general uneasiness about facial challenges that permeates the takings area should not apply, however, to *procedural* claims that deal with bias and judicial review. It would be appropriate to stay all arbitration proceedings until someone mounts a facial challenge against the interest-arbitration proceedings that could, and should, be handled on expedited judicial review.

The legal issues under the takings clause (and its close cousin, substantive due process)[26] are often subject to the argument that they should only be considered once they are ripe for reviews in individual cases. That position is doubtless correct under current law insofar as it applies to regulatory takings that only *restrict* the right of individuals to use and dispose of property of which they retain undisturbed possession.[27] The basic rules that govern these regulatory takings are highly plastic in that they take into account the particulars of the restrictions and the government justifications for their imposition, under a rational basis standard that is highly favorable to the government. In the famous formulation of

---

26. *See* Eastern Enterprises v. Apfel, 524 U.S. 498 (1998).

27. *See, e.g.*, Hodel v. Virginia Surface Mining & Reclamation Ass'n, 452 U.S. 264 (1981); Williamson County Regional Planning Commission v. Hamilton Bank, 473 U.S. 172 (1987); San Remo Hotel, L.P. v. City & County of San Francisco, 545 U.S. 323 (2005).

Supreme Court Justice Oliver Wendell Holmes, it is commonly held that government regulations do count as a taking if they "go too far," a standard that is elusive at best.[28]

In its modern formulation, the question is no longer whether the government has taken property, say in the form of air rights, but whether it has interfered with some "investment-backed expectations of individual landowners,"[29] which no one can quite define because of the evident circularity in this formulation. Expectations are supposed to determine the constitutionality of the law. Yet the law itself sets the relevant expectations, thereby creating the distinct possibility that an oft-repeated constitutional violation is insulated from attack simply because private landowners can anticipate its passage. On this view of the world, notice of the state's constitutional wrong is sufficient to deprive a landowner of his constitutional right.[30] Yet even that flexible test allows for successful challenges on an as-applied basis in some cases.[31]

The key point here is that however appropriate this framework is for the evaluation of the NLRA, it is wholly inapposite to the far greater intrusions of the EFCA, which should be evaluated on the per se takings rules that are used for physical takings under the current law.[32] Under that rule the size of the intrusion is only material to the level of damages that is awarded, but not to the existence

---

28. *See* Pennsylvania Coal v. Mahon, 260 U.S. 393, 415 (1922). "The general rule, at least, is that, while property may be regulated to a certain extent, if regulation goes too far, it will be recognized as a taking."

29. *See, e.g.,* Penn Central Transp. Co. v. City of New York, 438 U.S. 104, (1978). The often repeated formulation calls for an "ad hoc, factual inquiry" to evaluate the claim of a regulatory taking. The three questions asked are: (1) what is the economic impact of the regulation; (2) does the government action interfere with reasonable investment-backed expectations; and (3) what is the character of the government action. *Penn Central, 438 U.S. at 124.* For my criticism of these rules, see Richard A. Epstein, *Supreme Neglect: How to Revive Constitutional Protection for Private Property,* (Oxford Univ. Press, 2008).

30. For a decision that veers very close in that direction, *see* US Supreme Court, Monsanto, Co v. Ruckelshaus, 467 U.S. 986, 1006 (1984).

31. Philip Morris v. Inc. v. Reilly, 312 F.3d 24 (1st Cir. 2002) (government mandated disclosure of trade secrets a taking under *Penn Central*).

32. Loretto v. TelePrompter Manhattan CATV Corp., 458 U.S. 419 (1982) (cable box located on roof was a compensable taking).

of the taking. But why use that standard for physical takings in this case? The answer tracks the dominant distinction under current law that imposes the lower standards of rational basis on any rule that limits the ability of an owner to *use* its property as it sees fit, but the higher standard on any action that allows the government to *occupy* the land in question, or to authorize its occupation by others.

One key case in this regard is *Kaiser Aetna v. United States*, which holds that the highest level of protection is given to the right to exclude.[33] Accordingly, it held that the government could not condition the access of a marina to public waters on its owner's willingness to allow other boats in the harbor to use its waters. In contrast, zoning restrictions that prevent the construction of high-rises or require the preservation of open space restrictions on use are governed by a much more deferential standard of review. Even here the review is not completely idle. A rule that blocks all development needs a strong justification to survive.[34] Lesser restrictions still require that the owner retain some viable economic use of the property, albeit under standards that remain opaque to this very day.

This distinction between restrictions on use and government occupation is embedded in the current law. It can be challenged as a matter of general property theory, which affords the same level of protection to limited interests in property under the law of easements and restrictive covenants as it does to the outright ownership of land. But for these purposes, the constitutional deviation from private law theories of ownership is not to the point. What is critical is that the distinction between occupation and use maps perfectly into the difference between the original Wagner Act, as modified by the Taft-Hartley Act, and the EFCA. The current law regime limits the right of an employer to walk away from negotiations with the

---

33. Kaiser Aetna v. United States, 444 U.S. U.S. 164, 179 (1979).

34. *See* Lucas v. South Carolina Coastal Council, 505 U.S. 1003 (1992) (denial of permit to rebuild home on beachfront lot treated as a taking).

union, but does not force it to accept any particular contract that it found unacceptable. The union could not impose on the firm a losing arrangement that made it impossible for the firm to work with the union. That level of employer self-protection is what saves the NLRA from constitutional invalidation. Hence the parallel to land use restrictions. But the EFCA, by imposing a mandatory "first contract" arbitration scheme, forces the employer to accept a deal which is in no part of its making and in so doing to open its entire business (and trade secrets) to the union.

On this point too, Professor Gottesman errs by arguing that the limited framework of regulatory takings applies to these situations. But again he just misses the point. We can assume that the fractured law of regulatory takings would protect this statute if it applied. But the simple answer is that the wholesale requirement that the employer take on workers on terms that he does not accept calls for the application of the occupation paradigm. There is a vast difference between having to negotiate and being forced to accept a result that could create a disadvantageous contract, including one that could lead to bankruptcy.

As an analogy, the government violates the takings clause when it forces a landowner to sell property worth $100 in the open market to the government's designated buyer at the $75 price the government fixes. The forced sale leaves the owner short by $25, which difference the government has to make up. Otherwise, the willingness to pay a dollar to force the sale of the Empire State Building to a private party insulates the government from paying the full value to its owner. Likewise it is a taking to demand that an individual employer hire a worker for $100 per hour when the employer thinks that the labor is worth only $75. That is just what is happening here on a mass basis, given that compulsory arbitration offers no protection against the expropriation risk of forcing employers to pay far more for workers than they would voluntarily do. The state may without compensation set a minimum wage for workers.

But it cannot, without compensation, force the employer to hire workers at that wage when it does not wish to do so.

In response to this line of argument, it could be urged that other statutes force property owners to do business with others on unfavorable terms. Rent control statutes have long been held constitutional.[35] But surely these statutes would fail on constitutional grounds if the tenant were allowed to live on the premises for no rent at all. Indeed, as the law in this area has evolved, the current rent control statutes do not give the government complete freedom in setting the level of compensation that the landlord receives. The modern rule thus requires at the very least that the landlord be able to cover his costs, including all costs associated with the original acquisition of the property and its overall level.[36] That rule does not result in a per se invalidation of the EFCA that applies under the logic of *Loretto*, but it does imply that something akin to the rate of return analysis that is demanded in all rate-making cases be applied.[37] Any protection of this sort is absent here. It is possible that the Supreme Court—where this statute will surely end up—might imply what this statute clearly seems to deny, namely, an implied right of employers to mount judicial challenges against excessive arbitral awards. Unfortunately, this seems precluded by the last sentence of new Section 158(h)(3) that states baldly: "The arbitration panel shall render a decision settling the dispute and such decision shall be binding upon the parties for a period of two years, unless amended during such period by written consent of the parties." The term "binding" appears not only to preclude any appeal to an independent judicial tribunal, but also to deny that the arbitrator must make some initial findings that the firm could stave

---

35. *See* Block v. Hirsh, 256 U.S. 135 (1921).

36. Fisher v. City of Berkeley, 693 F.2d 261.294–295 (Cal. 1984) (requiring reasonable economic return on investment); Helmsley v. Borough of Fort Lee, 394 A.2d 65 (1978) (invalidating ordinance that limited rent increases to 2.5% for want of administrative relief in hardship cases).

37. *See* Duquesne Light Co. v. Barasch, 488 U.S. 299 (1989) (state has option to decide what form of rate of return regulation to impose).

off bankruptcy or continue to earn revenues that assure it a reasonable rate of return on invested capital, which other forms of rate-making generally require. Indeed, the statutory language contains no requirement for any written opinion explaining the reasons for the arbitral award. The precedents that truncate the constitutional protection for economic liberties do not apply to a statute that denies a regulated firm the ability either to exit from losing contracts or to obtain judicial review. The logic of EFCA to force down quick settlements comes at too high a constitutional price.

The want of any form of an exit right short of bankruptcy or liquidation dooms this statute under current constitutional principles. Think here of the comparisons to current law. No employer is required to hire a worker at the stipulated minimum wage, or to supply overtime work. EFCA takes that additional, and fatal, step. It stipulates the term of agreement without supplying either the option to withdraw or some guarantee of a reasonable rate of return after the arbitral decree is in force. For such draconian actions a higher standard of review seems appropriate—one that should invalidate the compulsory arbitration provisions of EFCA under current constitutional law principles.

CONCLUSION
WHAT SHOULD BE DONE?

I t is very difficult to critique the EFCA without undertaking a close examination of some of the defects of our current labor law system. EFCA only exaggerates its flaws. But what follows from that critique? In the current political and legal environment, there is no support for a return to the pre-Wagner Act days. Rather, the opponents of EFCA are determined defenders of the status quo, whatever their misgivings about the legal regime that regulates management-labor relations under the NLRA. Their position is that modern firms have learned to adapt to the present union environment and are able to deal with their workforce under the current law. They do not believe that all employers are insensitive dolts, who would rather fire a worker than learn from what he or she has to say. They believe that sound management practices and forward-looking workplace relationships can stave off unionization in any free and fair election. Their view is that the existence of unfair labor practices is a minor piece of the overall situation, to which all the provisions of EFCA, including its new sanctions of ULP, are overkill. EFCA's opponents also see this as a two-sided problem, given the eagerness of unions to resort to collateral attacks against employers through litigation and administrative complaints. They treat the decline of unionization in the private sector as stemming from the increased realization by workers that they are not on balance made better off by unions, whose fortress mentality cripples workers' prospects for advancement in today's global economy.[1]

Most of the time these defenders of the status quo are right. Workers who sign on to union representation tie their futures to an organization that need not represent their interests and that may not be nimble enough to make the needed adjustments in today's highly competitive global economy. Unions themselves acknowledge this point by their own behavior. They do not act as sales representatives who offer firms goods and services that their customers are only too happy to buy. Rather, they engage in multiple-front wars that involve litigation, administrative harassment, boycotts, pickets, and public denunciation to achieve their goals. The implicit claim in all this behavior—widely practiced but rarely acknowledged frankly—is this: you can be less worse off with the union than you are in the throes of an open-ended organization campaign. That strategy is no way to forge good working relationships or increase productivity.

Management representatives react to these new aggressive tactics with predictable hostility. The purpose of this extended essay is to explain what motivates their behavior, and why the status quo, with all its imperfections, will outperform any system that adopts card-check rules for union recognition and compulsory arbitration for a two-year "first contract," augmented by tougher penalties for employer ULPs. Legislation often promises grand improvements, only to be entrenched before its failures become evident. The correct presumption in all cases is that further legislation, being costly, has to be shown to be a good, or otherwise it should be treated as harm. EFCA does not come close to passing that test, which is why there are strong and principled reasons to oppose, and oppose vigorously, its passage.

---

1. For evidence in this direction, *see* Henry Farber and Bruce Western, *Round Up the Usual Suspects: The Decline of Unions in the Private Sector, 1973–1998*, 2 (Princeton University Industrial Relations Section Working Paper No. 437, 2000), *available at* http://papers.ssrn.com/sol3/papers.cfm?abstract_id=22981 0. *See also*, Michael Wachter, Labor Unions: A Corporatist Institution in a Competitive World, 155 U. Pa. L. Rev. 581, (2007).

Appendix

The Employee Free Choice Act

To amend the National Labor Relations Act to establish an efficient system to enable employees to form, join, or assist labor organizations, to provide for mandatory injunctions for unfair labor practices during organizing efforts, and for other purposes.

Be it enacted by the Senate and House of Representatives of the United States of America in Congress assembled,

SECTION 1. SHORT TITLE.

This Act may be cited as the 'Employee Free Choice Act of 2007.'

SEC. 2. STREAMLINING UNION CERTIFICATION.

(a) In General- Section 9(c) of the National Labor Relations Act (29 U.S.C. 159(c)) is amended by adding at the end the following:

'(6) Notwithstanding any other provision of this section, whenever a petition shall have been filed by an employee or group of employees or any individual or labor organization acting in their behalf alleging that a majority of employees in a unit appropriate for the purposes of collective bargaining wish to be represented by an individual or labor organization for such purposes, the Board shall investigate the petition. If the

Board finds that a majority of the employees in a unit appropriate for bargaining has signed valid authorizations designating the individual or labor organization specified in the petition as their bargaining representative and that no other individual or labor organization is currently certified or recognized as the exclusive representative of any of the employees in the unit, the Board shall not direct an election but shall certify the individual or labor organization as the representative described in subsection (a).

'(7) The Board shall develop guidelines and procedures for the designation by employees of a bargaining representative in the manner described in paragraph (6). Such guidelines and procedures shall include—

'(A) model collective bargaining authorization language that may be used for purposes of making the designations described in paragraph (6); and

'(B) procedures to be used by the Board to establish the validity of signed authorizations designating bargaining representatives.'.

SEC. 3. FACILITATING INITIAL COLLECTIVE BARGAINING AGREEMENTS.

Section 8 of the National Labor Relations Act (29 U.S.C. 158) is amended by adding at the end the following:

'(h) Whenever collective bargaining is for the purpose of establishing an initial agreement following certification or recognition, the provisions of subsection (d) shall be modified as follows:

'(1) Not later than 10 days after receiving a written request for collective bargaining from an individual or labor organization that has been newly organized or certified as a representative as defined in section 9(a), or within such further period as the parties agree upon, the parties shall meet and commence to bargain collectively and shall make every reasonable effort to conclude and sign a collective bargaining agreement.

'(2) If after the expiration of the 90-day period beginning on the date on which bargaining is commenced, or such additional period as the parties may agree upon, the parties have failed to reach an agreement, either party may notify the Federal Mediation and Conciliation Service of the existence of a dispute and request mediation. Whenever such a request is received, it shall be the duty of the Service promptly to put itself in communication with the parties and to use its best efforts, by mediation and conciliation, to bring them to agreement.

'(3) If after the expiration of the 30-day period beginning on the date on which the request for mediation is made under paragraph (2), or such additional period as the parties may agree upon, the Service is not able to bring the parties to agreement by conciliation, the Service shall refer the dispute to an arbitration board established in accordance with such regulations as may be prescribed by the Service. The arbitration panel shall render a decision settling the dispute and such decision shall be binding upon the parties for a period of 2 years, unless amended during such period by written consent of the parties.'.

SEC. 4. STRENGTHENING ENFORCEMENT.

(a) Injunctions Against Unfair Labor Practices During Organizing Drives-

'(1) Whenever it is charged—

'(A) that any employer—

'(i) discharged or otherwise discriminated against

an employee in violation of subsection (a)(3) of section 8;

'(ii) threatened to discharge or to otherwise discriminate against an employee in violation of subsection (a)(1) of section 8; or

'(iii) engaged in any other unfair labor practice within the meaning of subsection (a)(1) that significantly interferes with, restrains, or coerces employees in the exercise of the rights guaranteed in section 7;
while employees of that employer were seeking representation by a labor organization or during the period after a labor organization was recognized as a representative defined in section 9(a) until the first collective bargaining contract is entered into between the employer and the representative; or

'(B) that any person has engaged in an unfair labor practice within the meaning of subparagraph (A), (B) or (C) of section 8(b)(4), section 8(e), or section 8(b)(7);
the preliminary investigation of such charge shall be made forthwith and given priority over all other cases except cases of like character in the office where it is filed or to which it is referred.'.

(b) Remedies for Violations-

(1) BACKPAY- 'Provided further, That if the Board finds that an employer has discriminated against an employee in violation of subsection (a)(3) of section 8 while employees of the employer were seeking representation by a labor organization, or during the period after a labor organization was recognized as a representative

defined in subsection (a) of section 9 until the first collective bargaining contract was entered into between the employer and the representative, the Board in such order shall award the employee back pay and, in addition, 2 times that amount as liquidated damages: Provided further,'.

'(b) Any employer who willfully or repeatedly commits any unfair labor practice within the meaning of subsections (a)(1) or (a)(3) of section 8 while employees of the employer are seeking representation by a labor organization or during the period after a labor organization has been recognized as a representative defined in subsection (a) of section 9 until the first collective bargaining contract is entered into between the employer and the representative shall, in addition to any make-whole remedy ordered, be subject to a civil penalty of not to exceed $20,000 for each violation. In determining the amount of any penalty under this section, the Board shall consider the gravity of the unfair labor practice and the impact of the unfair labor practice on the charging party, on other persons seeking to exercise rights guaranteed by this Act, or on the public interest.'.

Index

Administrative Procedure Act (1946), 167
AFL-CIO. *See* American Federation of Labor and Congress of Industrial Organizations
agency shop, 100
  See also labor unions
American Federation of Labor and Congress of Industrial Organizations (AFL-CIO), 52
American Metal Products v. Sheet Metal Workers Local 104, 99
American Telephone and Telegraph (AT&T), 151, 151n57
anti-dumping action, 152, 152n62
arbitration, compulsory labor. *See* interest arbitration
arbitration, grievance, 81–82, 105, 117n15
arbitrator, EFCA
  bias of, 99, 102, 165–66, 168
  demand for, 109
  grievance arbitration and, 81–82, 105, 117n15
  guidance for, 109–10
  for panel, 83, 88–93, 94, 98, 181
  power of, 94, 98
  selection of, 82, 83, 88–93, 165–66, 181
association, political, card-check infringement upon, 157–58
AT&T. *See* American Telephone and Telegraph
at-will rule, 135–38

authorization cards. *See* card-check system
auto industry
  bailout for, 49, 62, 120
  transfer rights in, 120, 120n23
  union membership in, 119, 119n22, 121–22, 123
  See also individual automakers
autonomy, rights of, 159–60

bailout
  for auto industry, 49, 62, 120
  union contracts and, 120
ballot, secret
  card check *v.*, vii, 4–5, 19, 31, 43–48, 67
  elections by, 31, 43–48, 104
  employees and, 104
  for labor contract, 158
  NLRA and, 4
bankruptcy, 99, 155, 168, 173–74
bargaining, collective. *See* collective bargaining
benefits, company
  through arbitration, 103, 105, 114, 120, 131, 154
  by foreign/unregulated firms, 151
  as inducement, 38, 113, 130
  for nonunion employees, 142–43, 159
  pensions as, 42, 97–98, 113–14, 120, 126, 132
  for retirement, 120
  senior *v.* junior employees for, 120, 121
  as union advantage, 113, 125

About the Author

Richard A. Epstein is the Peter and Kirsten Bedford Senior Fellow at Hoover. He also holds an endowed professorship at the University of Chicago Law School, where he directs the Law and Economics Program. As of 2005, he has also been a visiting professor at New York University Law School. His areas of expertise include constitutional law, employment and labor law, intellectual property, and property rights. His most recent book is *Supreme Neglect: How to Revive the Constitutional Protection for Private Property* (Oxford, 2008).

In 2003 he was awarded an honorary degree in law from Ghent University. In 2005 he was named by *Legal Affairs* magazine as one of the twenty leading legal thinkers in the United States. Also in 2005, the College of William & Mary School of Law awarded him the Brigham-Kanner Property Rights Prize.

Epstein is known for his research and writing in a broad range of constitutional, economic, historical, and philosophical subjects. Among the subjects he has taught at the University of Chicago are administrative law, antitrust, communications law, constitutional law, contracts, corporation criminal law, employment discrimination law, environmental law, health law, jurisprudence, labor law, patents, property, torts, Roman law, real estate development and finance, and individual and corporate taxation.

He edited the *Journal of Legal Studies* (1981–91) and the *Journal of Law and Economics* (1991–2001). He is now a director of its Olin

Program in Law and Economics. He served as interim dean of the University of Chicago Law School in the spring of 2001. He has contributed articles to the *New York Times*, the *Wall Street Journal*, the *National Review*, and *Regulation* magazine. He writes a weekly column for Forbes.com and is a regular columnist for the Tech Forum on FT.com.

Epstein's books include *Supreme Neglect: How to Revive Constitutional Protection for Private Property* (2008); *How the Progressives Rewrote the Constitution* (2006); *Free Markets under Siege: Cartels, Politics and Social Welfare* (Hoover Institution Press, 2005); *Skepticism and Freedom: A Modern Case for Classical Liberalism* (2003); *Principles for a Free Society: Reconciling Individual Liberty with the Common Good* (1998); *Mortal Peril: Our Inalienable Right to Health Care?* (1997); *Simple Rules for a Complex World* (1995); *Bargaining with the State* (1993); *Forbidden Grounds: The Case against Employment Discrimination Laws* (1992); and *Takings: Private Property and the Power of Eminent Domain* (1985). Epstein is also the editor of *Cases and Materials in the Law of Torts* (9th ed., 2008) and has written a one-volume treatise, *Torts* (1999).

He received a B.A. degree in philosophy summa cum laude from Columbia in 1964. He received a B.A. degree in law with first-class honors from Oxford University in 1966 and an LL.B. degree, cum laude, from the Yale Law School in 1968. Upon his graduation he joined the faculty at the University of Southern California, where he taught until 1972. In 1972, he visited the University of Chicago and became a regular member of the faculty the following year. He was named James Parker Hall Professor in 1982 and Distinguished Service Professor in 1988.

He spent the 1977–78 year as a fellow at the Center for Advanced Studies in the Behavioral Sciences at Stanford University. He has been a senior fellow at the MacLean Center for Clinical Medical Ethics since 1984 and was elected a fellow of the American Academy of Arts and Sciences in 1985. He has been a Hoover fellow since 2000.